AF531476

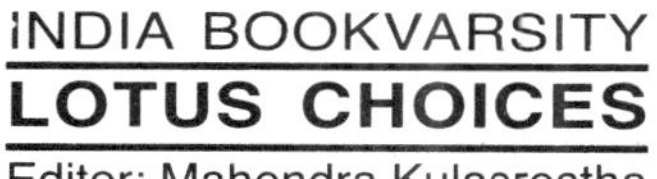

EVERYMAN'S BOOK OF HINDU RELIGION AND MYTHOLOGY

ABBE J.A. Dubois

Translated from the French
and edited by
Henry K. BEAUCHAMP,
Member of the Royal Historical Society
and Royal Asiatic Society

4735/22, Prakash Deep Building,
Ansari Road, Daryaganj,
New Delhi - 110002.

EVERYMAN'S BOOK OF HINDU RELIGION AND MYTHOLOGY

by

ABBE J.A. Dubois

Source: ***Hindu Manners, Customs and Ceremonies***
by Abbe J.A. Dubois
Published in 1816.

Everyman's Book of
Hindu Religion and Mythology

New First Edition—2012
ISBN: 978-81-8382-287-9 (H/B)

Published by:
LOTUS PRESS PUBLISHERS & DISTRIBUTORS
Unit No. 220, Second Floor, 4735/22, Prakash Deep Building,
Ansari Road, Darya Ganj, New Delhi-10002
Ph.: 011-23280047, 32903912 • Mob.: 098118-38000
E-mail: lotus_press@sify.com

Printed at: **Concept Imprint**, Delhi

EVERYMAN'S BOOK OF HINDU RELIGION AND MYTHOLOGY

by

ABBE J.A. Dubois

Source: ***Hindu Manners, Customs and Ceremonies***
by Abbe J.A. Dubois
Published in 1816.

Everyman's Book of
Hindu Religion and Mythology

New First Edition—2012
ISBN: 978-81-8382-287-9 (H/B)

Published by:
LOTUS PRESS PUBLISHERS & DISTRIBUTORS
Unit No. 220, Second Floor, 4735/22, Prakash Deep Building,
Ansari Road, Darya Ganj, New Delhi-10002
Ph.: 011-23280047, 32903912 • Mob.: 098118-38000
E-mail: lotus_press@sify.com

Printed at: **Concept Imprint**, Delhi

Editorspeak

Religion as Culture

Religion will not see the night of Time as long as the human-and-life-situation is not clarified. One may regard it as the greatest, along with God, invention of human beings in order to smoothen the sufferings of life—a basic that was discovered by the great Buddha so so long ago. Every community and country in the world has thought out its own religion; they are galore and come in an admirably large number of hues and shapes, propounding threories and promoting practices of mind-numbing varieties. There are one-book religions and many-many-books religions; religions believing in God as well as no-God at all; religions with philosophies as their basics and those with none at all; killing religions and non-killing ones and both verging on the extreme; idol-worshipping religions and idol-bashing ones; and so on and so forth. Here is a highly and truly surrealistic situation which will never be resolved.

India holds a very special place in this scenario. The mainstream current is known as Hindu, which happens to be a very large joint family of all kinds of religions, with lots and lots of philosophy and a fantastic culture of colour and shine and music and song. The most important feature of the Hindu group is that **it does not proseletyse**—the central cause of violence throughout history. No wonder, it is spreading essentially on its own in the fast waking up West, America in particular. The present pen-pusher was pleasantly surprised to read in the widely read American magazine, *Newsweek*, some time ago, when they described a situation somewhere in that vast land as being 'Hinduised' when the people did not take to arms in a religious matter, despite it being quite grave. I don't remember the details. Hindu Ahoy!

Hindu religion—as well as its sister, mythology—has for these reasons been a matter of great interest for foreigners: invaders in the early periods of history, the Muslim branch of whom mostly destroyed it to force their own religion, except for Dara Shikoh who got as many as sixty Upanishads translated into Persian, which, retranslated into Latin by Anquetil Duperron, reached France and then the whole of Europe through the famous philosopher Arthur Schaupenhauer; but the latter ones, the British, though they did bring their missionaries to convert the people to Christianity, though they did not succeed in their efforts beyond a very low point; and many of whom, including the famous F. Max Muller, became great admirers of the religion, its scriptures and philosophy. They wrote extensively on these subjects, translated many of the ancient books into English, German, etc., and, quite surprisingly, **declared that India cannot be converted to Christ's religion.**

The writer of the present work, the French missionary Abbe Dubois, who left his country in the wake of the French Revolution, and worked in India for three decades, in the South in particular, rues that he could succeed in converting hardly a couple of hundred Indians, most of them beggars, who did so for financial reasons. But he did one of the first major studies of Hindu society, its religion and culture, a huge work of over 800 pages, which was bought and published by the East India Company, and which is still a very authentic work on the subject. It was originally written in French, then translated into English, as well as edited by a scholar and published in the first decade of the last century.

As already indicated, it is an enoromous work, so the present editor has tried to restructure it into more than one volume of reasonable length on a few clear-cut subjects; this first one being limited to religion and mythology—the second one would perhaps be on sociology. Since times have changed, some of the text has been deleted; yet whatever remains provides a very interesting and quite detailed account of the conditions prevailing in those years.

Abbe Dubois, perhaps because he was a devoted Christian missionary, and that too from France, has been quite critical of many Hindu practices—some of his remarks I've deleted, and the editor Beauchamp also has in many places made comments in the footnotes—but in the end he does admire the role played by Hindu religion in keeping the very large number of communities—which he calls so many nations—together; and also in various places underlines the fact that the evil practices are limited to lower castes, Pariah and Sudras only—which should have been quite natural in view of their lack of education, etc.,—which happens to be the case even in modern times. In a few places he strongly criticises the Western practices also and holds them inferior to Hindu practices. Many of the details he has provided regarding the Hindu practices, are surprising to the Hindus also of modern times. I'm sure we of our country will also be greatly benefited by going carefully through this remarkable book.

Finally, Long Live Religion, and Hindu Religion in Particular, and let its family grow from national to global. Amen!

A Valuable Work

F. Max Muller

It is difficult to believe that Abbe Dubois, the author of *Moeurs, Institutions et Ceremonies des Peuples de l'Inde,* died only in 1848. By his position as a scholar and as a student of Indian subjects, he really belongs to a period previous to the revival of Sanskrit studies in India, as inaugurated by Wilkins, Sir William Jones, and Colebrooke. I had no idea, when in 1846 I was attending in Paris the lectures of Eugene Burnouf at the College de France, that the old Abbe was still living and in full activity as Directeur des Missions Etrangeres, and I doubt whether even Burnouf himself was aware of his existence in Paris. The Abbe belongs really to the eighteenth century, but as there is much to be learnt even from such men as Roberto deNobili, who went to India in 1606, from H. Roth, who was much consulted by Kircher in his *China Illustrata* (1667), and others, so again the eighteenth century was by no means devoid of eminent students of Sanskrit, of Indian religion, and Indian subjects in general.

It is true that in our days their observations and researches possess chiefly a historical interest, but they are by no means to be neglected. They make us see how the acquaintance of European scholars with India began, and under what circumstances the first steps were taken by these pioneers, chiefly missionaries, towards acquiring a knowledge of the ancient language of India, Sanskrit, and through it, towards gaining an acquaintance with one of the most interesting peoples and one of the richest and most original literatures of the world. The reports sent from India by Pere Coeurdoux (1767), and published by Barthelemy in the *Memoirs of the French Academy*, the letters of Pere Calmette (1733), and of Pere Pons (1740), are full of curious information, anticipating on many points the later discoveries of Sir William Jones and other members of the Asiatic Society of Bengal. It should be remembered also that the first Sanskrit grammar was published at Rome in 1790 by Paolino de S. Bartolommeo, four years before the death of Sir William Jones (1746-1794).

Abbe Dubois, though born about 1770 and therefore considerably the junior of Sir William Jones belonged by his place in the history of Sanskrit scholarship to the period that came to an end with the beginnings of the Asiatic Society of Bengal, which had been founded by Sir William Jones in 1784. Nor must it be forgotten that while the real revival of Sanskrit studies took place in Bengal, Abbe Dubois spent the whole of his life in the Deccan and in Madras Presidency. He was, therefore, as may be seen by his translation of the *Panchatantra*, under the title of *Le Pantchatantra ou les cinq ruses*, Fables du Brahme Vichnou-Sarma; *Aventures de Paramarta et autres contres*, le tout traduit pour la premiere fois, Paris,

1826, a Tamil far more than a Sanskrit scholar, and well acquainted with Tamil literature, which hitherto has been far too much neglected by students of Indian literature, philosophy, and religion.

Though little is known of Abbe Dubois' life beyond the fact that he lived retired from the world, and retired even from his fellow-workers, and a stranger, it would seem, to the researches which were carried on all around him by the devoted and enthusiastic scholars of Sanskrit literature in France, England, and Germany, his principal book, *Description of the Character, Manners, and Customs of the People of India, and of their Institutions, Religious and Civil,* published both in French and in English, has always continued to be read and to be quoted with respect, as containing the views of an eye-witness, of a man singularly free from prejudice, and of a scholar with sufficient freedom from prejudice and of a scholar with sufficient knowledge, if not of Sanskrit, yet of Tamil, both literary and spoken, to be able to enter into the views of the natives, to understand their manners and customs, and to make allowance for many of their supersitious opinions and practices, as mere corruptions of an originally far more rational and intelligent form of religion and philosophy.

New men who were real scholars have hitherto undertaken to tell us what they saw of India and its inhabitants during a lifelong residence in the country, and in spite of the great opportunities that India offers to intelligent and observant travellers, we know far less of the actual life of India than of that of Greece and Rome. There are few men now left who, like Abbe Dubois, have actually been present at the burning of widows, or who can give us, as he does, the direct reports of eye-witnesses who saw a king burnt with two of his queens joining hands on the burning pile over the corpse of their husband. In the South these Suttees were far less frequent than in Bengal, where in the year 1817 no less than 706 cases of Suttee had been officially reported, and where this practice had at last to be put down by the law during the Governor-Generalship of Lord William Bentinck (1825-1835), thanks chiefly to the active exertions and the moral influence of Ram Mohun Roy.

As a trustworthy authority on the state of India from 1792 to 1823 Abbe Dubois' work will always retain its value, and in its final and complete form now offered to the public, it will be welcome not only to Sanskrit scholars, but to all who take an intelligent interest in that wonderful country. As the Abbe went to India as a missionary, and was a man remarkably free from theological prejudices, missionaries in particular will read his volume with interest and real advantage.

Abbe Dubois and His Book

Henry K. Beauchamp

In the Library of the Madras Literary Society and Auxiliary of the Royal Asiatic Society may be seen, in a conspicuous position above one of the doorways, a striking portrait in oil-colours. This portrait at a distance one takes to be that of some Hindu, clothed in white, wearing a white turban, and holding in one hand, the bamboo staff that tradition assigns to a Hindu pilgrim. A closer inspection, however, shows that in reality it is the portrait of a European, a face that literally speaks to you from the canvas.

This portrait is that of Abbe J.A. Dubois, a Christian missionary who laboured for some thirty-one years in India, striving to fulfil the task which his sense of religious duty imposed upon him. Merely in this respect one can claim for him no special merit. His special claim to recognition will be found elsewhere, in the wonderful record which he compiled of the manners, customs, institutions, and ceremonies of the people among whom he lived and moved.

In his day, it must be remarked, there were no royal roads to such knowledge. There were no text-books to prepare the way by their critical analyses of the sacred Hindu writings. Such knowledge had to be gained at first hand, and by the more laborious method of personal inquiry in situ.

'I had no sooner arrived amongst the natives of India,' the Abbe himself tells us, 'than I recognized the absolute necessity of gaining their confidence. Accordingly, I made it my constant rule to live as they did. I adopted their style of clothing, and I studied their customs and methods of life in order to be exactly like them. By such conduct I was able to ensure a free and hearty welcome from people of all castes and conditions, and was often favoured of their own accord with the most curious and interesting particulars about themselves.'

Major Mark Wilks, the accomplished historian of Mysore, who in those days was British Resident in that province, in introducing the Abbe's work to the notice of the Government of Fort St. George, remarked: 'Of the history and character of the author, I only know that he escaped from one of the fusillades of the French Revolution and has since lived amongst the Hindus as one of themselves; and of the respect which his irreproachable conduct inspires, it may be sufficient to state that when travelling, the house of a Brahmin is uniformly cleared for his reception, as a spontaneous mark of deference and respect.'

The Abbe was ordained in the diocese of Viviers in 1792, at the age of twenty-seven, and left France in the same year. On reaching India he was attached to the Pondicherry Mission. He must have quickly made for himself a name, for on the fall of Seringapattam, he was specially invited to visit the capital of Mysore in order to reconvert and reorganize the Christian community which had been forcibly perverted to Mahomedanism by Tippu Sultan. I may mention that, through the influence of the Abbe in Mysore, not a single priest of the Missions Etrangeres was persecuted by Tippu. He once more gathered the lost sheep, and established on a permanent basis the Roman Catholic Church in the province of Mysore. **He met the problem of the poverty of the people committed to his care by founding agricultural colonies and he used his influence to such good effect in preventing epidemics of small-pox by promoting vaccination—** then, a comparatively novel idea—that he was afterwards granted a special pension by the East India Company.

The French MS. of the work which the Abbe compiled has a somewhat remarkable history. In its original form it was placed in the hands of Major Wilks in the year 1806, when the Abbe had been some fourteen years in the country. Major Wilks studied it for more than a year and then forwarded it to the Government of Fort St. George with a letter of warm recommendation. This judgement was heartily endorsed by Sir James Mackintosh, and also by Mr. W. Erskine, of Bombay, a man of distinguished talents and an acknowledged authority in everything connected with the mythology, literature, customs and institutions of the people of India. Major Wilks had no difficulty in persuading Lord William Bentinck, who was then at Madras, to purchase the MS. on behalf of the East India Company.

The purchase of the MS. was reported by the Madras Government to the Board of Directors in 1807 as 'an arrangement... of great public importance'; and the MS. itself was transmitted to London at the same time for translation and publication. It was not until 1816, however, that the English translation was actually published.

As to the intrinsic value of the Abbe's work, I have no hesitation in saying that it is as valuable to-day as ever it was, even more valuable in some respects. It is true that a mass of learned literature on the religious and civil life of the Hindus has accumulated since the Abbe's days, but the fact is that the Abbe's work, composed as it was in the midst of the people themselves. is of a unique character, for it combines, as no other work on the Hindus combines, a recital of the broad facts of Hindu religion and Hindu sociology with many masterly descriptions, at once comprehensive and minute.

There is one other matter which I feel bound to refer to before concluding, and that is the impression he derived after three decades of Mission labour as to the possibility of converting India to Christianity. I have no wish to renew the bitter controversy which ensued on the publication of his *Letters on the State of Christianity in India* soon after his return of France; the purport of those *Letters*, as I understand them, was to assert that, **under existing circumstances, there is no human possibility of converting the Hindus as a nation to any sect of Christianity.**

He refers to the collapse of the Church, with its hundreds of thousands of converts, many of them of high caste. The Abbe completely despaired of the higher castes ever becoming Christians, though he was ready to acknowledge that there was a harvest-field among the low castes and outcastes. On his own attempts to convert the Hindus he remarks: 'For my part I cannot boast of my successes. During the long period I have lived in India in the capacity of a missionary, I have made with the assistance of a native missionary, in all between two and three hundred converts of both sexes. Of this number two-thirds were Pariahs or beggars; and the rest were composed of Sudras, vagrants, and outcastes of several tribes, who being without resource, turned Christians in order to form connexions, chiefly for the purpose of marriage or with some other interested views.'

It may be mentioned that in the agricultural settlement of reconverted Christians the inhabitants retained their Hindu caste distinctions; and the following observations in Mr. V.S. Narasimha Iyengar Mysore Census Report (1891) are noteworthy:

'Roman Catholicism is able to prevail among the Hindus by reason of its policy of tolerating among its converts the customs of caste and social observances, which constitute so material a part of the Indian social fabric. They still pay worship to the Kalasam at marriages and festivals, call in the Brahmin astrologer and purohita, use the Hindu religious marks, and conform to various other amentities.'

The last years of the Abbe's life were spent at the headquarters of the Missions Etrangeres at Paris. He left India on January 15, 1823. On his return to Paris he was at once made Director of the Missions Etrangeres, and from 1836 to 1839 he filled the post of Superior. During his leisure he found time to translate into French the whole of the *Panchatantra,* the famous book of Hindu fables, and also a work which he entitled *The Exploits of the Guru Paramarta.* He died in 1848 at the patriarchal age of eighty-three.

Madras, Sept. 1897

Authorspeak

Authentic Records

Though Europeans have possessed settlements in India for more than three centuries, it is only within recent times that authentic details have been obtained with respect to the people who dwell in this vast country and whose ancient civilization, methods of government, manners, creeds and customs, are nevertheless so well worthy of notice. **It is impossible to doubt for a moment at an epoch when our most civilized countries of the West were still plunged in the dark abyss of ignorance, the various forms of their institutions, both political and social; their knowledge of mathematics, especially of astronomy; their systems of metaphysics and ethics: all of these had long ago made the people of India famous far beyond their own borders; while the renown of Hindu philosophers had reached even Europe.**

The many ill-informed and often contradictory narratives about India which have been published in present times have deservedly fallen into discredit. Yet it must be admitted, some good work has been done by certain literary societies that have of recent years been established in India. Yet, it must be confessed, the information which we possess about the people of India is very meagre. The ancient history of their country is, for one thing, enshrouded in chimera and fable, that it is not too much to presume that we shall never succeed in throwing proper light on all this mass of absurdities.

My readers will see in the following pages to what extremes the people of India carry their belief in and love for the marvellous. Their first historians were in reality poets, who seem to have decided that they could not do better than compose their poems in the spirit of the people for whom they were writing. The Indian muse of history thus became a kind of magician whose wand performed wonders.

While waiting for inquirers more skilful than myself, to find a way through this labyrinth, which to me is absolutely inextricable, I offer to the public a large number of authentic records which I have carefully collected and which, for the most part, contain particulars that are either unknown or only partially known. I believe, that they will be acknowledged to contain some useful materials for future savants who may undertake a complete and methodical treatise on the people of India.

In this new edition the contents of my first MS. have been carefully revised and corrected. They have, moreover, been considerably augmented by many curious details which did not appear in the original document. During my long sojourn in India I never let slip any opportunity of collecting materials and particulars of all sorts. My information has been drawn partly from the books which are held in highest estimation amongst the people of India, and partly from such scattered records as fell by chance into my hands and contained facts upon which I could thoroughly rely. But in regard to the majority of the materials, I am chiefly dependent on my own researches, having lived in close and familiar intercourse with persons of every caste and condition of life.

In publishing these records of my researches I have no wish to aspire to literary fame. I have noted down just what I saw, just what I heard, just what I read. I have aimed only at simplicity and accuracy.

Contents

1. The Principal Gods
♋ 25-42 ♋

2. Trimurti: Brahma, Vishnu, and Siva
♋ 60-79 ♋

3. The Worship of Animals
♋ 80-98 ♋

4. Inanimate Gods of Worship
♋ 97-105 ♋

5. The Doctrine of Metempsychosis
♋ 106-122 ♋

6. The Jain Religion
♋ 123-147 ♋

7. Mantras, Sandhya, Sacrifices
♋ 148-182 ♋

8. Priests and Purohitas
♋ 183-204 ♋

9. The Hindu Sects
♋ 205-237 ♋

10. Hindu Temples
♋ 238-277 ♋

11. Hindu Festivals
♋ 278-289 ♋

12. Hindu Feasts
♋ 290-302 ♋

13. Principal Ceremonies
♋ 301-318 ♋

1

The Principal Gods

Surely no one will expect me to relate here the histories of all the inferior deities which swarm in Hindu mythology; a mere catalogue of them would fill a large volume; and much more numerous still are the strange stories that Hindu legends contain about them. Only the gods of the first order can find a place here.

Among those of the highest rank are first of all Brahma, Vishnu, and Siva. Sometimes, under the name of the Trimurti, these three gods receive the homage of their devotees in common; at other times each one is the object of particular worship. From these again have sprung a multitude of others, whom the Hindus, faithful to their practice of exaggeration, reckon up to the astounding total of three hundred and thirty millions. I will only refer to the most renowned of these, and I believe that my readers will thank me for sparing them the greater part of the details which the people of India attach to these gods, and which amount with them to articles of faith. Let us begin with the deity occupying the first rank in this extensive hierarchy.

Brahma[1]

According to tradition, Brahma issued originally from a lotus flower. He was born with five heads; but he outraged Parvati, the wife of Siva, and Siva avenged himself by striking off one of the heads of the adulterous god in single combat. Consequently, Brahma is now represented with only four heads, and he is often called the four-faced god.

He rides on a swan, and his emblem is a water-lily. His own daughter, Sarasvati, is his wife. Having conceived for her an incestuous passion, and not daring to satisfy it under the human form, he assumed that of a stag, and changed his daughter into a hind. It is for

1. 'The more common name for the one Spirit is Atman or Paramatman, and in the later system, Brahman, neut. (nom. Brahma), derived from root *brih*, "to expand," and denoting the universally expanding essence or universally diffused substance of the universe. It was thus that the later creed became not so much monotheistic (by which I mean the belief in one God, regarded as a Personal Being external to the universe though creating and governing it) as pantheistic; Brahman in the neuter being "simple infinite being"—the only real eternal essence—which, when it passes into universal manifested existence, is called Brahma; when it manifests itself on the earth, is called Vishnu, and when it again dissolves itself into simple being, is called Siva; all the other innumerable gods and demigods being also mere manifestations of the neuter Brahman, who alone is eternal. This, at any rate, appears to be the genuine pantheistic creed of India at the present day.' —Monier-Williams.

having thus violated the laws of nature that he has, so they say, neither temple nor worship nor sacrifice. Some pundits maintain, however, that the feeling of indifference evinced towards Brahma is caused by the malediction cast upon him by a certain penitent named Bunumi, who, on presenting himself for admission to the Abode of Bliss, was received with irreverence by the god. But whatever may be the motive, it is an accepted fact that Brahma does not anywhere receive public worship.

They allow him, however, three attributes of high importance: for he is (1) the author and creator of all things; (2) the dispenser of all gifts and favours; and (3) the sovereign disposer of the destiny of man.

At the creation of mankind the Brahmins, the most noble of all men, sprang from his head, the Kshatriyas issued from his shoulders, the Vaisyas from his stomach, the Sudras from his feet. This, at any rate, is the version most commonly recognized; but it is denied by some authors, who say that Brahma created a first man, who was the father of all the rest. Brahma made him first of all with only one foot; but seeing that he had difficulty in moving about in this form, Brahma destroyed his work, and made another with three feet: at last perceiving that this third foot was like a fifth wheel to a coach, Brahma began his labour over again, and made man with two feet.

It is through Brahma in his quality of supreme disposer that the other gods, the giants, and certain other privileged creatures, have obtained the privileges and prerogatives which they enjoy. Brahma can even confer immortality, as he has done in the case of some famous personages, such as the giants Ravana, Hiranya and several others.

By reason of the sovereignty which Brahma exercises over the destinies of mankind, all men are born with their fates written on their foreheads by the hand of the god himself. This destiny is absolute and irrevocable. It embraces five principal objects, namely, length of life, disposition, intelligence, worldly condition, and virtuous or vicious inclination. What Brahma has predestined in all these is inevitable and must be strictly fulfilled. The Hindus are so fully convinced of this that in all adversities and troubles of life they are heard to exclaim: 'Thus was it written on my forehead!' If they are called upon to sympathize in the troubles of a relative or friend, they never omit to utter this consolatory saying: 'No being can escape that which is written on his forehead!' Thus, in all cases where a Christian would exclaim with humble resignation, God's will be done, they say with an equal resignation, What is written on the forehead must be fulfilled. It is also upon this irrevocable and irresistible destiny that Hindus lay the faults and crimes committed by them. Instances of

this are constantly occurring in the courts of justice now established in the country. Thus, when judges ask criminals what has brought them to commit the crimes for which they are convicted, they invariably respond, 'Thus it was written on my forehead, and it was not in my power to avoid it.[1]'

Each man is also endowed with one of the three qualities namely, goodness or truth (*satva*), passion (*rajas*), and ignorance (*tamas*). Whichever of these qualities has fallen to a man's lot is inherent in his being, and is in conformity with his deeds in previous existences; it influences him in all the actions of his life.

This doctrine of fate or destiny was recognized in heathen antiquity from the earliest times. It was the subject of speculation among Greek and Roman philosophers; and, as we all know, there are philosophers of modern times who have felt no shame in adopting it. However, the wisest of the Greek a Roman philosophers correctly gauged the consequences of attributing such an influence to destiny, an influence which, by depriving men of all liberty, destroys both virtue and vice, and constitutes God the Author of all crime. In other terms, that is to say, it disturbs the basis of all morality and of all religion.

---

1. This was the excuse offered by a Hindu who was a few years ago charged with the murder of his mistress at the Mazagon Police Court, Bombay, for the sake of her jewels.

Vishnu

One of the commonest names of Vishnu in the southern part of the Indian peninsula is Perumal. His devotees are fond of invoking him under the name of Narayana; and he has a thousand other names, of which the Brahmins have composed a species of litany which they call Hari-smarana.

The worship rendered to Vishnu, the sign of the *namam*, which his followers trace on their forehead, is the distinctive symbol of that worship. His cult is more general than that of Siva, especially among the Brahmins, whose favourite god appears to be Vishnu.

He is represented with four arms, and hence is sometimes named the four-armed god. The bird garuda is his vehicle. He bears the title of redeemer and preserver of all that exists. The other gods, not excepting Brahma himself, have often had need of his help in escaping from perils which threatened them. In his quality of preserver he has found himself obliged to take different forms, which the Hindus designate under the name of Avatars or incarnations. Of these they count ten principal ones, the nomenclature of which is contained in the following verses:

Adau matsyas tatah kurma Varahascha param tatah

Narasimha maha sakti vamanascha param tatah

Ramascha Balaramascha Parasustadanantaram
Kalkirupascha Baudhascha hyavatara dasa smitah.

1. Matsya-avatar, in the form of a fish;
2. Varaha-avatar, in the form of a pig;
3. Kurma-avatar, in the form of a tortoise;
4. Narasimha-avatar, in the form of a monster, half man and half lion;
5. Vamana-avatar, in the form of a Brahmin dwarf, named Vamana;
6. Parasurama-avatar, in the form of Parasurama;
7. Rama-avatar, in the form of the famous hero known as Rama;
8. In the form of Bala-rama;
9. Buddha-avatar, in the form of Buddha;
10. Kalki-avatar, in the form of a horse.

There is yet another famous incarnation, which is that of Vishnu in the person of Krishna, without counting many others; and all these, if I am not mistaken, originally possessed an allegorical meaning, the object being to prove the all-pervading presence of the divinity. For instance, one reads in the Bhagavata:

'One day, the penitent Arjuna having invoked Vishnu with favour and devotion, and having prayed him to reveal himself to him, this powerful god, who has deigned to manifest himself to man under all kinds of forms, answered him thus: "These, Arjuna, are the forms in which thou must above all invoke me,

acknowledging them as part of my divine essence:

'In prayer, I am the Gayatri.
'In speech, I am the word Aum.
'Among the gods, I am Indra.
'Among the stars, I am the Sun.
'Among the hills, I am Mount Meru.
'Among the Rudras, I am Sankara.
'Among the rich, I am Kubera.
'Among the elements, I am Fire.
'Among the purohitas, I am Brihaspati.
'Among the generals of armies, I am Kartika.
'Among the penitents, I am Bhrigu.
'Among the sages, I am Kapila-Muni.
'Among the Gandharvas, I am Chitraratha.
'Among the weapons, I am the Thunderbolt.
'Among the birds, I am the Garuda.
'Among the elephants, I am Airavata.
'Among the cows, I am Surabhi.
'Among the monkeys, I am Hanuman.
'Among the serpents, I am Ananta.
'Among the waters, I am the Sea.
'Among the rivers, I am the Ganges.
'Among the trees, I am the Aswattha.
'Among the shrubs, I am the Tulasi.
'Among the grasses, I am the Darbha.
'Among the stones, I am the Salagrama.
'Among the giants, I am Prahlada.
'Among the months, I am Margasirsha.
'Among the learned books, I am the Sama-Veda.

'In short, I am the spirit of all that exists; I permeate the universe.'

The Kalki-avatar, or horse incarnation, has not yet occurred, but it is expected, although the time and place where it will happen are not known. It will put an end to the kingdom of sin, which began with the Kali-yuga.

Vishnu will then appear in the form of a horse; he will be of gigantic stature; he will be armed with a huge axe; his voice will resemble the rolling of thunder, the noise of which will spread terror everywhere. First he will destroy all kings, then all other men. Finally, seeing that his father and mother are but sinners like the rest of mankind, he will sacrifice them also to appease his anger. After this a New Age will begin, when virtue and happiness will reign on the earth.

If one may believe certain learned Brahmins whom I have had an opportunity of consulting on this subject, it would appear that the incarnation of Buddha has also not yet taken place. It ought to have occurred at the beginning of the Kali-yuga in the country called Kitoki. This Buddha will preach pure atheism to mankind: he will lead even the gods themselves into sin and error. In these unhappy times Sudras will be seen wearing red cloths, a colour which is only meant for Brahmins, and acquiring knowledge, the Vedas not excepted. So little virtue will then be practised on the earth that what there is will not suffice to render man happy in this world or the next. The Brahmins will no longer fulfil the duties of their calling, will hold in no esteem the rules concerning defilement and cleanliness.

Children will no longer obey their parents; there will be no more caste distinctions; even kings will practise all that is most vile and contemptible among men. Earth itself and the other elements will feel the effects of the universal disorder which will then prevail in nature; the former will lose, at any rate partially, its fertility; little rain will fall from the clouds; the cows will yield but little milk, and that, moreover, will not be fit for making butter.

In the opinion of most Brahmins, however, the Avatar in question has already taken place. They cannot exactly fix its date, but they maintain that it is this Avatar which put an end to the bloody sacrifices formerly in vogue.

It is probable the same epoch witnessed the establishment of Buddhism, which prevails throughout the greater part of Asia, but has been almost entirely destroyed by the Brahmins in India. Be this as it may, it is certain that under this Avatar the Brahmins render no homage to Buddha or to Vishnu.

I must mention in conclusion the famous incarnation of Vishnu in the person of Rama, which forms the subject of the celebrated epic poem known as the Ramayana, the most famous of all Indian books, and read by persons of all castes.

Rama

Rama, or the incarnation of Vishnu under this name, was the son of Dasaratha, King of

Ayodhya, his mother was Kausalya. He spent the first years of his life in the jungles under the guidance of the penitent Viswamitra. It was there that, touching with his feet Ahalya, who had previously been turned into stone by a penitent's curse, he restored her to life and to her original form.

Subsequently he went to the court of Janaka, King of Mithila. This prince, having witnessed several of his deeds of prowess, proposed to him that he should break the bow of Siva, which until then none of the kings of the earth had been able to do. Rama accomplished this task with ease, and won Sita, daughter of the King of Mithila, as the reward of his strength and valour. Hardly had the marriage been celebrated when Rama's father recalled him, and entrusted him with the reins of government. After returning to his paternal home he was one day practising with his bow, and shot an arrow with such force that its twang as it left the bow caused an abortion in a Brahmin woman who was pregnant. The husband, in a transport of rage, uttered this curse:—'May Rama henceforth possess no more knowledge than the rest of men!' The curse had its effect, and from that time Rama was deprived of the divine knowledge inherent in him. Shortly after this event, Kaikeyi, the fourth wife of Dasaratha, earnestly desiring to obtain the crown for her own son, visited Rama and implored him with the most urgent entreaties to forego his claims. This Rama consented to do, and after abdicating he retired

once more into the jungles, accompanied by his brother Lakshmana and his wife Sita.

One day while Rama was afar off in the forests, Lakshmana cut off the ears of Surpanakha, sister of the ten-headed giant Ravana, King of Lanka, who, indignant at the insult offered to his sister, avenged himself by carrying off Sita. Rama, learning on his return of the misfortune which had befallen him in his absence, was prostrated with grief, and could think of nothing but the means of rescuing his beloved Sita from the clutches of her ravisher. In order to succeed in his design, he began by making an alliance with Sugriva, king of the monkeys, to whom he rendered great service by killing Bali, his brother, who had long contested the empire with him and was then in possession of it.

Impatient for news of his wife, Rama determined to send someone to Lanka without further delay, to obtain information. The undertaking was not easy, as there was an arm of the sea to cross. But Hanuman, son of the Wind and commander-in-chief of the army of monkeys, whom Sugriva had sent to help his ally Rama, was endowed with extraordinary agility, which seemed to render him the most appropriate person for such an embassy. He was therefore appointed to the task. He started, crossed the straits, walking dry-shod over the surface of the waters, and arrived at Lanka. After a long and unsuccessful search, Hanuman at last discovered Sita sitting in a solitary spot under a shady tree, plunged in

the deepest grief, and watering the ground with her tears, while her sobs alternated with curses at her sad fate. At one time she would load Ravana with maledictions, at another she would utter the most poignant regrets at the separation from her beloved Rama, to whom she swore inviolable fidelity, whatever efforts her treacherous ravisher might employ to seduce her.

Hanuman hurried back and told Rama all he had seen and heard. Rama at once conceived the idea of constructing a dam across the straits to make a passage for his army. The monkey Hanuman, entrusted with this great undertaking, set to work to uproot mountains and rocks. At each journey to the straits he carried as many stones as he had hairs on his body, and piling them up on one another, had soon achieved his task of joining the island of Lanka to the continent.

Rama, however, thinking himself hardly strong enough to attack his formidable enemy with the army of monkeys, formed a second army of bears, and with this reinforcement he prepared to cross the straits. Before setting out he placed a lingam on the dam, and offered a solemn sacrifice to it. Then, turning towards his armies of bears and monkeys, he addressed them as follows:

'Brave soldiers, do not let yourselves be frightened by the giants against whom you are to wage war; their strength is useless, since

the gods are not on their side: Let us advance, then, without fear and without delay. We march to certain victory, since we go to fight the enemies of the gods.'

At these words the whole force moved forward, crossed the straits, invaded Lanka, engaged in several battles with the giant Ravana, and after many vicissitudes of victory and defeat, at last gained the upper hand for Rama. Ravana was vanquished and killed; and Sita, the cause of this terrible war, was rescued and carried off in triumph to her own country of Ayodhya.

On leaving Lanka, Rama placed on the vacant throne Vibhishana, Ravana's brother[1], in recognition of the great services which he had rendered during the war, and before departing promised he should wear the crown as long as the world lasted, that is, as long as the name of Rama should exist.

Some time after his return to Ayodhya, Rama, having one night left his palace in disguise to find out what was going on in the city, overheard at a street corner some words uttered by a washerman quarrelling with his wife, of whose faithfulness he seemed to have conceived strong suspicions. In his anger the washerman declared that he would drive her from his house, telling her that he was not the man to keep a wife—as Rama did—who had

1. Vibhishana was a younger brother of Ravana. He was a noble-minded rakshasa, or giant unlike the other giants.

been in the power of another. These words fell like a thunderbolt on Rama, who, full of rage and grief, hastened back to his palace. He at once sent for his brother Lakshmana, told him what he had heard, and ordered him to seize Sita, take her far away into the jungles, and put her to death.

Lakshmana immediately set about executing his brother's orders. However, as Sita was far advanced in pregnancy, he had scruples about killing her in this condition, and resolved to save her life. The difficulty was to invent some stratagem in order to persuade Rama that he had executed the task entrusted to him. Now it happened that in the jungles to which Sita had been taken there were several trees which, as soon as an incision was made in the bark, emitted a juice the colour of blood. Lakshmana accordingly bent his bow, and taking the arrow which had been destined to pierce Sita's heart, shot it into one of these trees, staining it with the juice, and then abandoned Sita to her unhappy fate. He at once returned and announced to Rama that his vengeance had been satisfied, and for proof of it showed him the arrow stained with Sita's blood[1].

Alone and abandoned in this deserted place, poor Sita proclaimed her despair in mournful cries and torrents of tears. It

1. In memory of this event it is customary on the last day of the military feat of the Dasara for princes to go with great ceremony into the open country and there shoot off arrows.

happened that Valmiki, a penitent, had made his dwelling-place not far off. Attracted by the weeping and wailing which struck his ear, he approached Sita, and asked her who she was and what was the cause of her trouble. The unfortunate woman thereupon stopped her sobs, and assuming an air of dignity which filled the penitent with respectful fear, answered him thus: 'I am Sita! The king Janaka is my father, the Earth is my mother, and Rama is my husband.'

At these words the penitent, filled with the most profound feelings of veneration, prostrated himself before the goddess; then, rising and clasping his hands, he said to her:

'Illustrious goddess, why give yourself up thus to grief and despair? Have you forgotten that you are the queen and mistress of the world, and that on you the salvation of all creatures depends?'

He spoke a few more words of consolation, and then led her to his hermitage, where he offered sacrifices to her.

A few days afterwards Sita brought forth twins, which the penitent Valmiki reared with as much care as if they had been his own children.

Now it came to pass subsequently that Rama resolved to perform the great sacrifice or yajna, Rajasuya, and let loose the horse which was intended for the victim. The animal, after passing through many countries, came to the place where the two sons of Sita dwelt; and they, full of strength and courage, though at that time only five years of age, intercepted and stopped him.

The monkey Hanuman, general of Rama's armies, was accordingly sent with a considerable force to fight against the sons of Sita and to recover the horse; but Hanuman was vanquished by them, and compelled to seek safety in flight.

Rama, at the news of this disaster, placed himself at the head of his whole forces, and went in person to attack his new enemies. But he in his turn was defeated by the sons of Sita, and he and his soldiers were cut to pieces, not one escaping. Valmiki was informed of this occurrence, and proceeded to the field of battle, which he found literally strewn with the dead. Touched with compassion for Rama and his troops, he pronounced over them the mantra which restores life, and raised them all from the dead.

Rama returned home, and determined to perform once more the great sacrifice to which he invited all the neighbouring kings and all the illustrious Brahmins of the country. But the latter, on being consulted as to the best means of making the sacrifice complete, answered that it could not be so unless Rama's wife was beside him. After raising many difficulties, Rama at last consented to recall her, and to all appearances gave her a hearty welcome.

Consequently, the sacrifice of the horse was a complete success. But Rama thereupon wished to repudiate his wife anew, and to send her back to the jungles. All the kings present interceded in her behalf. Still Rama would not yield to their entreaties, except on the condition that she proved, by subjecting herself to the ordeal of fire, that her virtue had not suffered any taint.

Sita, conscious of her innocence, issued from the ordeal with honour and glory, and from many others not less searching; yet, in spite of all, she could not cure her husband of his odious suspicions and unjust jealousy.

Overwhelmed at last with confusion and shame, she burst into a flood of tears, and in the extremity of her despair she addressed the following prayer to her mother:

'O Earth! thou to whom I owe my existence, justify me this day in the sight of the universe; and if it is true that I have never ceased to be a virtuous woman, accord me an indisputable proof of my chastity by opening thyself under my feet and swallowing me up!'

No sooner had she uttered these words than the Earth, in response to her prayer, opened and swallowed her up alive within her bosom.

Rama did not tarry long before following his spouse. Having divided his kingdom between his two sons, he retired to the banks of the Sarayu, where he lived for some time in retirement and penance, and then closed his mortal career.

Krishna

The history of Krishna, or of Vishnu under this name, is told in many Puranas. The eighteenth, the Bhagavata, deals with him almost exclusively. I will give a very short analysis of this.

In the Jambudwipa is a country called Bharatvarsha. In this country is Brindavana, or paradise of Krishna, which is the supreme paradise; where untold delights are to be enjoyed. It is larger than Swarga, and the beauty of it is beyond all description.

It is inhabited by an infinite number of shepherds, the chief of whom is Nanda, Krishna's foster-father. On the north of Brindavana is the town of Mathura where Ugrasena reigned. He was expelled from his kingdom by his son Kansa, who seized the throne and indulged for a long while in innumerable acts of injustice and unheard-of cruelty.

The Earth, unable to bear this tyrant's violence any longer; took the form of a cow, went in search of the four-faced Brahma, and having done him homage, spoke as follows:

'O Creator of all things, it is to you that I owe my being; it is your duty therefore to protect me. The king Kansa, who has given himself up altogether to sin, holds me in the most cruel oppression. I can bear his tyranny no longer. This wicked man is your creature. Therefore, issue orders to him and forbid his injuring me further.'

Brahma, angered at this report, went with the supplicant to Siva, and told him what he had learnt. All these next went together to Vishnu, the Supreme Being; and after they had offered their respectful salutations, the cow—that is, the Earth still in this form—spoke thus:

'Great god, you always listen graciously to the prayers addressed to you. I come, then, in my unhappiness to implore your protection. Kansa, the cruel Kansa, is committing the most unheard-of cruelties against me. I prostrate myself at your feet, and beg of you to put an end to them by slaying this evildoer.'

After listening to these complaints, Vishnu asked Brahma whether he had not formerly granted some special favour to this Kansa, and what was its nature.

'The favour which I granted him,' answered Brahma, 'is that he can only be deprived of life by his own nephew. Enter, therefore, into the womb of Devaki, his sister; for there is no other way of getting rid of this tyrant.'

So Vishnu followed Brahma's advice, and became incarnate in the womb of Devaki, sister of Kansa and wife of Vasudeva, one of the most celebrated merchants of the country.

Kansa, on learning all that was going on, placed guards and spies everywhere, thrust Vasudeva and his wife into close confinement, and loaded them with fetters. However, Devaki was not long in giving birth to Krishna, and

the day of his birth was the eighth of the moon of the month Sravana. Being informed that Kansa had resolved to kill the child, Devaki managed to escape the vigilance of the guards and had him secretly carried away into the town of Gokula.

At the same time Yasoda, wife of the shepherd Nanda, had given birth to a daughter. To prevent this cruel design of Kansa the two children were interchanged. Yasoda, who had sunk into a deep slumber during the birth of her child, had been unable to ascertain whether she had given birth to a boy or a girl; she did not therefore detect the substitution, and always looked upon Krishna as her own son.

As soon as the tyrant Kansa had learnt of his sister's safe delivery, he ordered the child to be brought to him so that it might be put to death. But the child, an incarnation of the Supreme Being, was already in safety at Gokula in the house of the shepherd Nanda. Kansa wished, but in vain, to vent his rage on the little girl, who was no less than the Supreme Being himself under the name of Bhadra-Kali, whose adventures are to be found written in the history of the goddesses.

Little Krishna spent his earlier years in games and amusements suitable to his age. His ordinary pastime was to steal milk and butter, which was divided afterwards with his friends the shepherds. His youth was thus spent in the midst of a pastoral life, and he is often

represented playing on a flute, the favourite instrument of shepherds.

In the meanwhile he declared war against the tyrant Kansa, his uncle, routed and slew him, and gave back the crown to Ugrasena.

Having resolved to marry, he carried off the maiden Rukmani and very many other virtuous girls. The number of his wives amounted to sixteen thousand.

He waged several wars against demons, against the king Banasura, and even against Siva himself, who had sided with the latter monarch. It was Aniruddha, Krishna's son, who caused the dispute between his father and Banasura, whose daughter Usha he (Aniruddha) had attempted to carry off. The ravisher was kept prisoner for a long time, and was only given back to his father after several long and bloody battles. Krishna, after rescuing his son, began to build in the middle of the sea the town called Dwaraka, and took his family there.

At length, having seen all his children die before his eyes, he himself paid tribute to nature. The victim of a curse, which a penitent in his wrath had pronounced against him, he fell pierced by a huntsman's arrow.

The following are some of the principal blessings which the world gained from this incarnation of Vishnu in the person of Krishna:

He put to death Pootana, a woman celebrated for her extraordinary size, strength, and ferocity.

He effaced from the earth a great number of giants. He uprooted two trees of such tremendous size that they covered one-half of the earth with their shade.

He chastised the serpent Kaliya.

He suspended a mountain in the air to serve as an umbrella for forty thousand shepherds who had been overtaken by a storm.[1]

Besides all this, he cut to pieces Kansa and all his followers.

However, this is enough about the incarnations of Vishnu. Others before me have spoken at great length about him. I will merely repeat that, judging by the outward worship paid to him, this god must be considered as disputing the highest rank with Brahma.

To Vishnu are attributed five weapons called by the common name of Panchayudha. But the two principal ones are the Sankha, which he holds in his left hand, and the Chakra, which he holds in his right.

Siva

This god is also called Ishwara, Rudra, Sadasiva, Mahadeva, Parameswara, and a host of other names. He is represented under a horrible form, in allusion no doubt to the power which he possesses of destroying everything. He is made to appear still more frightful by having his body covered with ashes. His long hair is plaited in a strange manner; his eyes of

1. The mountain on that account was called Govardhanagiri.

huge size make him appear to be in a constant state of fury. Instead of jewels his ears are adorned with snakes, which are likewise twined round his body. There are some colossal idols representing Siva which are calculated to inspire genuine terror.

The principal attribute of this god is the power of destruction. Some Hindu authors ascribe to him also the power of creation. His vehicle is a bull, and his principal weapon is the trident or *trisula*.

The history of Siva, like that of the other Hindu deities, is a tissue of the most extravagant fables. It consists of endless wars waged by him against the giants, of his hatred and jealousy towards the other gods, and, above all, of his intrigues.

In one of his wars, wishing by an unexpected attack to accomplish the ruin of all his enemies, the giants, and to take possession of the Tripura in which they had entrenched themselves, he split the earth into two equal parts, and took one-half as a weapon. He made Brahma the general of his army; the four Vedas served him for horses. Vishnu was used as an arrow, while Mandara Parvata served as a bow. In place of a bow-string he tied to his bow a monstrous serpent. With this formidable equipment Siva led his army against the enemies of the gods, took from them the three fortresses which they had constructed, and exterminated them all without sparing a single one.

Siva had much trouble in finding a wife; but having done a long and austere penance in the deserts bordering on Mandara Parvata, Parvata was so touched that he finally contented to give him in marriage his daughter Parvati.

The Lingam

The Lingam, an object of deep veneration throughout India, is the symbol of Siva, and it is under this obscene form that the god is principally honoured. One finds in several Puranas details of the origin of the superstitious worship of which it is the object. However much these details may vary, as to the main point the story is everywhere the same. Here, in abridged form, is what the Linga-purana says:

Brahma, Vishnu, and Vasishta, accompanied by the numerous following of illustrious penitents, went one day to Kailasa the paradise of Siva to pay a visit to the god, and surprised him with his wife. He was not in the least disconcerted by the sudden presence of the illustrious visitors, and showed no shame at being discovered in such a position.

The fact was that the god was greatly excited by the intoxicating liquors which he had drunk, and at the sight of him some of the gods, and especially Vishnu, began to laugh; while the rest displayed great indignation and anger, and loaded Siva with insults and curses. They said to him, 'Behold, thou art but a devil, thou art worse even than a devil! Thou hast the form of one, and dost possess all the

wickedness! We came here in a spirit of friendliness to pay thee a visit, and thou dost not blush to make us spectators of thy sensuality! Be accursed! Let no virtuous person from henceforth have any dealings with thee! Let all those who approach thee be regarded as brutes, and be banished from the society of honest folk!'

After pronouncing these curses, the gods and the penitents retired, covered with shame. When Siva had recovered his senses a little, he asked his guards who it was that had come to visit him. They told him everything that had taken place, and described to him the angry attitude that his illustrious friends had assumed.

The words of the guards fell on Siva and his wife Durga like a clap of thunder, and they both died of grief in the same position in which the gods and the penitents had surprised them. Siva desired that the act which had covered him with shame, 'and which had been the cause' of his death, should be celebrated among mankind.

'My shame,' said he, 'has killed me; but it has also given me new life, and a new shape, which is that of the lingam! You, evil spirits, my subjects, regard it as my double self! Yes, the lingam is I myself, and I ordain that men shall offer to it henceforth their sacrifices and worship. Those who honour me under the symbol of the lingam stall obtain, without fail, the object of all their desires, and a place in

Kailasa. I am the Supreme Being, and so is my lingam. To render to it the honours due to a god is an action of the highest merit. The Bilva tree is, of all trees, the one I love the best. If anyone wishes to obtain my favours, he must offer me the leaves, the flowers, and the fruit thereof. Hear once more, evil spirits, my subjects. Those who fast on the fourteenth day of the moon of the month Magha in honour of my lingam, and those who, on the following night, do puja, and present to me leaves of the tree, shall be certain of a place in Kailasa.

'Hear yet again, evil spirits, my subjects. If you desire to become virtuous, learn what are the benefits to be derived from honour rendered to my lingam. Those who make images of it with earth or cow-dung, or do puja to it under this form, shall be rewarded; those who make it in stone shall receive seven times more reward, and shall never behold the Princes of Darkness; those who make it in silver shall receive seven times more reward than the last named; and those who make it in gold shall be seven times more meritorious still.

'Let my priests go and teach these truths to men, and compel them to embrace the worship of my lingam! The lingam is Siva himself; it is white; it has three eyes and five faces; it is arrayed in a tiger's skin. It existed before the world, and it is the origin and the beginning of all beings. It disperses our terrors and our fears, and grants us the object of all our desires.'

It is incredible that in inventing this superstition the religious teachers of India intended that the people should render direct worship to objects the very names of which, among civilized nations, are an insult to decency. Without any doubt the obscene symbol contained an allegorical meaning, and was a type in the first instance, of the reproductive forces of nature, the generative source of all living beings. For the rest, the lingam offers an incontestable analogy to the priapus of the Romans and the phallus of the Egyptians.

One sees figures of the lingam, not only in the temples dedicated to Siva, but also on the high-roads, in public places, and other frequented spots.

Vighneshwara

This divinity bears also the names of Ganesa, Pillayar, Vinayaka, etc. He is venerated by Hindus of all sects, and his cult is universal. One comes across his idol everywhere—in temples, schools, *chattrams*, public places, forts, on the high-roads, near wells, fountains, tanks; in short, in all frequented places: It is taken into houses, and in all public ceremonies Ganesa is always the first god to be worshipped. He is, and as his name implies, the god of obstacles, and by reason of this a Hindu begins every serious undertaking by seeking to propitiate him.

He is represented under a hideous form, with an elephant's head, an enormous

stomach, and disproportioned limbs, and with a rat at his feet. Siva was his father, and Bhadra-Kali, or Durga, his mother. He is said to have given himself up entirely to a life of meditation, and to have never married.

The first time that his mother Bhadra-Kali saw him, she reduced his head to ashes by the brilliancy of her look. Siva, on learning this misfortune, and being sorely grieved at having a son without a head, considered earnestly how he might provide him with this eminently useful member. With this intent he sent his servants with orders to cut off the head of the first living creature they met sleeping with the face turned towards the north, and to bring it to him. An elephant happened to be the first creature they perceived in this position, and following Siva's instructions they cut off the animal's head, and hurried back with it to their master. Siva took it and fitted it on his son's neck, and since then Ganesa has preserved the shape under which he is still represented.

The elephant's head, and also the rat, are probably emblems of the prudence, sagacity, and forethought which the Hindus attribute to this divinity.

Indra

Indra is the king of the gods of the second rank, who live with him in Swarga. He is the son of Kasyapa and Aditi. The inferior gods and the virtuous persons who inhabit his happy domains are without number.

To make them happy Indra distributes *amrita* (nectar) to them, and allows them to enjoy all the pleasures of the senses, to which he also gives himself up without restraint; there is no kind of sensual enjoyment that cannot be indulged in, without satiety, in Swarga.

Indra's vehicle is an elephant, and his weapon the Vajra, a kind of sharp knife. Lightning is also his weapon in his wars against the giants.

Ashta Dikpalas

Indra occupies the first rank among the eight Dikpalas, who preside over and guard the eight principal divisions of the world. The following table will explain all that is interesting about these divinities, who are placed by the Hindus after the gods of the first rank:

Names	Position of their kingdoms	Their chargers	Their weapon	Colour of their garments
Indra	East	An elephant	The vajra	Red
Agni	South-east	A ram	The sakti	Violet
Yama	South	A buffalo	The danda	Orange
Nairuta	South-west	A man	The yellow	Dark
Varuna	West	A crocodile	The pasa	White
Vayu	North-west	An antelope	The dhwaja	Blue
Kubera	North	A horse	The khadga	Pink
Isana	North-east	A bull	The trisula	Grey

Those who seek for analogies between the gods of India and those of Greece may remark certain striking similarities. Like the Greek gods, each Hindu god has a particular weapon, and also a particular animal sacred to him.

Abodes of Bliss

There are four Abodes of Bliss: Swarga, Kailasa, Vaikuntha, and Satya-loka. The first is Indra's paradise, the second Siva's, the third Vishnu's, and the fourth Brahma's.

In describing these pleasant retreats, the Hindu books represent Mount Mahameru, on the slopes of which they are situated, as being in the form of a cone, convoluted like a snail's shell and divided into stages. On the first, on the north side, is Swarga, Indra's paradise; to the left, on the east side and at the next stage, is Kailasa, Siva's paradise; at a still higher stage, on the south side, is Vaikuntha, Vishnu's paradise; and, finally, on the summit of the mountain is Satya-loka, Brahma's paradise.

Swarga

Indra's paradise is inhabited by the gods of the second rank, who are all children of Kasyapa, and of his first wife Aditi. The palace of Indra, their eldest son, and king of this realm of delight, is in the centre, sparkling with gold and precious stones. There is also another palace of equal splendour for Sati, his wife, Puloma's daughter. Their son is Jayanta. In this paradise grows the famous kalpa-tree, the golden fruit of which has an exquisite flavour;

and there also is the cow Kamadhenu, which gives delicious milk. This fruit and milk form the nourishment of the gods.

The kalpa-tree and Kamadhenu the cow are held in high esteem by the Hindus, and are referred to on almost every page of their books. The kalpa-tree, which grows to the height of ten yojanas, has the power of satisfying all the desires of men who put their trust in it. As for Kamadhenu the cow, she is not less prodigal of her bounties, and can, among other things, grant milk and butter in abundance to anybody who invokes her with sincere faith and devotion. Many other trees are to be found in Swarga, while the limpid waters of many rivers meander there in all directions, the principal one being the Mandakini. The eyes of the inhabitants of this happy abode are refreshed by the rhythmical and voluptuous movements of throngs of dancing-girls; while the sweet notes of the vina, which the Gandharvas, famous musicians, play in accompaniment to their melodious songs, charm the ear without ceasing. Innumerable courtesans, too, are always ready to satisfy the passions which they excite. Brihaspati performs the office of guru to the gods in Swarga, and explains the Vedas to them. Finally, strangely enough, two duly appointed physicians are to be under there, Asvini Kumara. The Ashta-Dikpalas, mentioned above, hold the first rank, as is natural, among the inhabitants of this Abode of Bliss. The nine

planets also have their abode there, and it is from thence that they shine upon us. The seven famous penitents, or munis, and an infinite number of other saints are the habitual guests of Indra.

Entrance to Swarga is granted to all virtuous persons, without exception, of whatever rank or caste, provided they have attained on earth the required degree of sanctity.

Kailasa

Above Swarga is a city constructed on a triangular plan. It is called Kailasa. It is a charming place. Siva rules over it, and it is here that he resides with his wife Parvati. They are both depicted as giving themselves up continually to carnal pleasures. Ganesa and Kartika are their sons, both of whom are endowed with extraordinary strength. Ganesa, the elder, devotes himself exclusively to meditation; Kartika cares for nothing but weapons, and thinks of nothing but war.

Siva's courtiers are a band of evil spirits, of whom Nandi is the chief. His lieutenants are Bhringi, Bhima, and Kadurgita, all of whom have terrible countenances. Bhairava, Bhima, and Darshana are charged with the care of the city, which is peopled with various kinds of evil spirits, horrible to behold, which spread terror everywhere. He is clothed in a tiger's skin covered with ashes, and his body is entwined with serpents. Seated on his ox, he rides occasionally on the neighbouring mountains

with his wife Parvati. The demons who form their escort utter piercing cries, terminating with a shriek like *kill kill* and it is from this that Kailasa takes its name. The paradise of Kailasa is reserved for the followers of Siva, the worshippers of the lingam.

Vaikuntha

Vaikuntha is the paradise of Vishnu, reserved for those who are specially devoted to the worship of this god. It is above Kailasa, and occupies a most charming site; hence the name Vaikuntha, signifying 'Pleasant.' Gold and precious objects of all sorts sparkle on every side. In the midst of this enchanting abode rises a superb palace inhabited by Vishnu and his wife Lakshmi; close to them are Pradyumna, their eldest son, and a host of other children, their grandson Aniruddha, son of Pradyumna, and Usha, his wife, and their daughter Bana. In this abode, as in the rest, there are flowers, trees, quadrupeds, birds, and especially peacocks in great numbers.

The river Viraja flows below the royal residence. Many penitents live on its banks, and there spend happy, peaceful days; their food consists of fruits and vegetables, which grow without cultivation; their leisure is divided between reading the Vedas and meditating.

Satya Loka

The name of Satya Loka signifies 'The Place of Truth,' or 'The Abode or Virtue.' Satya Loka is the highest of the Abodes of Bliss. It is the paradise of Brahma, where he lives with his wife Sarasvati. The Ganges waters this divine retreat, and it is hence that some of its purifying waters have reached the earth. It is reserved for those Brahmins only who, by the practice of virtue on earth, have arrived at the degree of sanctity necessary to gain admittance thereto. Persons of any other caste, however edifying and pure their lives may have been, are irrevocably excluded from it.

2

Trimurti: Brahma, Vishnu, and Siva

The Hindus understand by the word Trimurti the three principal divinities whom they acknowledge. These are Brahma, Vishnu, and Siva. The word properly signifies 'the three powers,' viz., Creation, the special attribute of Brahma; Preservation, the attriute of Vishnu; and Destruction, the attribute of Siva.[1]

These three divinities are represented sometimes singly with their special emblems, and sometimes joined together in a single body with three heads. It is under the latter form that they obtain the name of Trimurti, which means, at once, both the three bodies and the three powers. This union of persons is the allegorical symbol of the existence of things created, which can neither be produced nor

---

1. The first is the religion of activity and works; the second, that of faith and love; the third. that of austerity. contemplation, and spiritual knowledge. This last is regarded as the highest, because it aims at entire cessation of action and total effacement of all personal entity and identity by absorption into simple Soul.

—Monier-Williams.

preserved without the agreement and the sanction of these three powers.

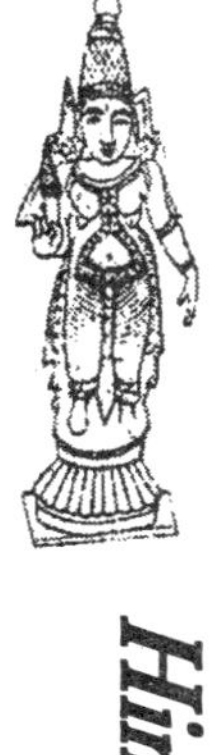

The Trimurti is recognized and worshipped generally by all Hindus except the Jains. Although many Hindus are specially devoted, some to Siva and others to Vishnu, nevertheless when these two divinities are united with Brahma in a single body with three heads, they all pay equal worship to the three without regard to the particular points of doctrine which otherwise separate them.

It is very difficult to trace the origin of the Trimurti inasmuch as the accounts of it do not agree. In some Puranas it is related that the Trimurti sprang from a female source called Adi Sakti the original power, who gave birth to these three divinities united in a single body; and it is added that after having brought them into the world she fell so desperately in love with them that she married them.

In some other Puranas we read that Adi-Sakti produced a seed front which was born Siva, the father of Vishnu.

Elsewhere we are told that a flower of the Tamarasa plant (water-lily) sprang from the navel of Vishnu, and that from this flower Brahma was born.

In short, we find in the Hindu books a mere tissue of contradictions relating to the Trimurti, and the details which are related in connexion with each are even more inconsistent. The point on which they agree

to a certain extent is that which relates to the excesses and the amours of the three divinities composing it.

In spite of the great power which these divinities enjoyed, they were, nevertheless often compelled to feel the terrible vengeance of virtuous persons, who, shocked at the sight of their infamous proceedings, found means of reducing them to subjection and, inflicting on them severe punishment. Thus, for example, there was a certain virgin, named Anasooya, who was as much renowned for her inviolable chastity as for her devotion to the gods and for her tender compassion for the unfortunate. The divinities of the Trimurti, having heard of her, became so greatly enamoured that they resolved upon robbing her of her virginity, which she had till then treasured with so much care.

To attain their object the three seducers disguised themselves as religious mendicants, and under this guise went to ask alms of her. The virgin came to them, and with her wonted kindness showered gifts upon them. The sham beggars, after being loaded with her gifts, told her that they expected from her another favour, which was to strip herself naked before them and to satisfy their desires. Surprised and frightened by this shameful proposal, she repulsed them by pronouncing against them certain mantras. These, together with some holy water which she poured upon them, had the effect of converting them into a calf. After they had been thus transformed, Anasooya

took upon herself to bring up this calf by feeding it with her own milk.

The Trimurti remained in this humiliating position till all the female deities combined together and, fearing lest some great misfortune might befall them in the absence of their three principal gods, after consulting one another, went in a body to Anasooya and begged her most humbly to give up the Trimurti and to restore them to their former state. It was with great difficulty that Anusooya was persuaded to yield to their prayers, and even then she imposed a condition that they should first of all be ravished, by whom the fable does not say. The female deities, convinced that they could not otherwise rescue the Trimurti, consented to undergo the penalty required of them, choosing rather to lose their honour than their gods. The conditions being fulfilled, Anasooya restored the Trimurti to their former state, and they returned to the place whence they came.

This scandalous adventure of the mighty divinities of the Trimurti is one of the least indecent of the kind in the Hindu books. But whatever may be the confusion pervading the contradictory accounts of the different Puranas, I am inclined to believe that all that is said about the three divinities of the Trimurti, and of the follies which are ascribed to them, is a mere mass of allegory.

At the commencement of their idolatry the Hindus confined their worship to visible

objects, such as the sun, the moon, the stars, and the elements. In those early times they felt no need of making idols of stone, wood, or metal. But as paganism extended its dominion, and when, in imitation of other idolatrous nations, the Hindus went so far as to deify simple mortals, they had recourse to statues and images in order to perpetuate the memory of their celebrated men and to transmit their virtues to posterity. By degrees, with the same object in view, they gave a bodily form to all the objects of their worship. The origin of the Trimurti dates, I believe, from a period long after the establishment of idolatry in India.

It may justly be presumed that this symbolic representation of the three divinities united in a single body denotes merely the three elements which are most perceptible to all, earth, water, and fire. In course of time the original notion vanished, and an ignorant people, guided solely by the impression of the senses, gradually converted what was at first a simple allegory into three distinct and real divinities.

Comparing with Greek Gods

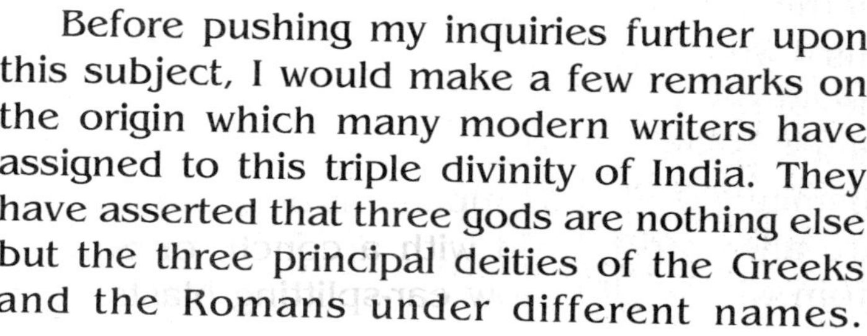

Before pushing my inquiries further upon this subject, I would make a few remarks on the origin which many modern writers have assigned to this triple divinity of India. They have asserted that three gods are nothing else but the three principal deities of the Greeks and the Romans under different names.

Brahma, according to them, is Jupiter, Vishnu is Neptune, and Siva is Pluto. In fact, according to the mythology of the Greeks, Jupiter is the author and the creator of all things; he is the father, the master, and the king of gods and men. Now, all these attributes belong equally to Brahma. The Hindus say that the universe is the egg of Brahma, and that after laying it, he hatched it. He also particularly resembles Jupiter in his incestuous alliances. Jupiter had for his wife Juno, his sister; Brahma is, at the same time, the father and the husband of Sarasvati; and it would be easy to enumerate many more points of resemblance between these two divinities.

The resemblance between Neptune and Vishnu is no less striking. Neptune makes the waters his abode; the sea is his empire; there he reigns, mounted on his chariot in the form of a shell drawn by sea-horses, and armed with his formidable trident. He is attended by Tritons, who make the whole sea re-echo with the sound of their conches. One of the most common names for Vishnu is Narayana, which signifies one that sojourns in the waters. He is represented as quietly sleeping on the surface of the ocean. It is true he has neither trident in his hand nor Tritons around him; but his devotees bear or their forehead a symbolic figure which closely resembles a trident, and in imitation of the companions of Neptune, they are always provided with a conch, or Sankh, from which they blow ear-splitting blasts, and

the figure of which is also stamped on their shoulders with hot iron.

Siva, again, is a perfect prototype of Pluto, the gloomy god of hell, the lord of the shades and of night. To Siva belongs the power of destruction. He it is who reduces everything to dust; he takes delight in giving vent to his sobs and groans in places of burial, whence he derives the name of Rudra commonly given him. It signifies one who causes lamentation.

Pluto, unable to find a woman willing to dwell with him in his dismal abode, carried off Proserpine, and concealed her so well that for a long while she escaped the search of her mother Ceres. In like manner, Siva found a wife in a remote quarter. Unable to get one elsewhere, he obtained one at last from the mountain Mandara, who gave him in marriage his daughter Parvati, in consideration of a long and severe penance which Siva endured for her sake in the deserts.

But though some features of resemblance lead us to believe in the identity of the fabulous deities of India with those of Greece and Rome, we find ourselves disconcerted at every step. As a matter of fact both Vishnu and Siva, as well as Brahma, possess many traits of likeness to the Olympian king. It was Vishnu who cleared the earth of a multitude of giants that overran it—giants who far exceeded in stature Enceladus, Briareus, and the other Titans who were destroyed by Jupiter. Jupiter is borne by

an eagle; Vishnu likewise rides a pretty eagle called Garuda, which, though the smallest of the birds of its own species, became enormously large when it carried the god under the designation of Jagannatha, i.e., Master of the World, an attribute which he shares with the most powerful of the sons of Saturn.

Juno is the goddess of wealth. The name of Lakshmi, the wife of Vishnu, also signifies one who gives riches. Jealous like Juno, Lakshmi had a good deal to suffer, as well as her prototype, on account of the infidelities of her husband. The Romans, in the fasts which they celebrated in honour of their gods, always represented Jupiter in company with his wife; and the Hindus do the same in the case of Vishnu and Lakshmi.

There are other divinities, such as Devendra, Varuna, and Yama, who display still greater resemblances to the three most powerful deities of Greek mythology. Devendra, whose name is equivalent to that of master of the deities, is the 'monarch of the sky.' He exercises his sovereignty over the deities of the second rank, who inhabit with him a place called Swarga, where they enjoy all kinds of carnal pleasures. He distributes among them the amrita, which has the virtue of rendering them immortal. Like Jupiter, he is armed with lightning and launches it against the giants.

Varuna is really the Hindu Neptune. He is the god of water, the lord of the ocean, and is worshipped as such over the whole Peninsula.

We recognize Pluto in Yama. Yama exercises his sovereignty in Naraka (hell), as Pluto does in Tartarus. He presides at men's death-beds, and determines their subsequent destiny according to the deeds, good or bad, which they have done during their lifetime. I might prolong this comparison, without however drawing the conclusion that the Hindus ever borrowed their system of theogony from the Greeks, or the Greeks from the Hindus.

But if it is not from other ancient peoples that the Hindus derived their three principal divinities, whence have they derived them? I shall attempt some reflections on this point with all the reserve imposed upon me by a subject so difficult of explanation. Let us first observe that Hindu idolatry differs in one essential point from that which prevailed formerly in Athens and in Rome. In Greece and Rome it was not the sea that was worshipped, but its monarch, the god Neptune. All his attendants, the Nereids and the Tritons, had a share in the worship offered to him. It was not to the forests, to the rivers, or to the fountains that prayers were offered, but to the Fauns and to the Naiads who presided over them.

The idolatry of India has for the object of its worship the material substance itself. It is to water, to fire, to the most common household implements; in a word, to everything which they understand to be useful or hurtful, that the Hindus pay direct worship.

It is true that they admit another kind of idolatry. There are images of deities of the first rank which are exposed to public veneration only after a Brahmin had invoked and incorporated in them these actual divinities. In these cases, it is really the divinity that resides in the idol, and not the idol itself, that is worshipped.

But the one kind of worship does not exclude the other; and that which has for its object the actual substance itself is the most common. The Hindus hold, as an invariable principle, that every object, animate or inanimate, which has the power of doing good or evil, should be worshipped.

'My god,' a respectable Hindu said to me one day, 'is the headman amongst my field labourers; for as they work under his orders, he can, by using his influence, do me much good or much evil.'

I have somewhere read a conversation between the wives of the seven famous Rishis, in which they agreed in the principle that the chief god of a woman is her husband, by reason of the good or evil he can do her; and we have already seen that the rules of conduct drawn up for Hindu ladies continually remind us of this idea. It is this same notion which makes the Hindus attach so much importance to the blessing or the curse of persons reputed to be saints; it is on the same principle also that they are so easily persuaded to give the name of god to princes and great personages, and, in

short, to everyone from whom they have something to hope or to fear.

The rage for deifying everything has spread even to the mountains and to the forests. The savage tribes who inhabit these places do not worship any of the gods of the country; they have one special deity of their own: it is a big root; a sort of potato, which grows abundantly in the forests, and forms their principal staple of food. Knowing nothing more useful than this vegetable, they make it the object of their worship. In its presence they celebrate their marriages, and in its name they take their oaths.

Earth, Water, Fire

Probably the Trimurti owed its origin to this mode of viewing objects. Earth, water, and fire were the types of the three divinities which compose it. The earth is the common mother of all things, animate and inanimate. Either they spring from her bosom, or they live upon her productions. It is through her that everything subsists in nature. She has, therefore, been regarded as the divine creator, and holds the first rank in the opinion of the Hindus, who have made her their Brahma.

But what could the earth do without the help of water? Without the dews and the rains which develop the seeds of her fertility she would remain barren, and would soon find herself bereft of every living creature. It is water which gives life, preserves, and causes to grow everything that has life or vegetates. It was,

therefore, regarded as the divine preserver, that is to say, Vishnu.

Fire, in penetrating the other two elements, communicates to them a portion of its energy, develops their properties, and brings everything in nature to that state of growth, maturity, and perfection which would never be arrived at without it. But, should it cease to act upon created things, everyone of them perishes. When it is in its free and visible state, this active agent of reproduction destroys by its irresistible power the bodies to whose composition it had before contributed; and it is to this formidable power that it owed its title of god-destroyer, that is to say, Siva.

By uniting the three elements in a single body with three heads the founder of the Hindu theology wished it to be understood that the harmony of these three primal elements was indispensable to the production and reproduction of all secondary bodies.

This is not a theory of my own merely for the purpose of explaining the original idolatry of the Hindus; it is their own peculiar doctrine, observed by them in daily practice. It is even one of the fundamental tenets of the religion of the Brahmins.

The Brahmins offer worship and address mystical prayers to the seven inferior worlds, of which the first and the most important is the earth. 'Glory to thee, O earth, mother most great,' are the words of the Yajur-Veda; and

immediately after is added: 'Glory to thee, O fire, who art god.'

There is no surer proof that they attach to fire itself the idea of divine essence than their perpetual sacrifices of homa and of yajna, in which no other object of worship than this element is observable.

The divinity of water is also incontestably recognized as an article of their belief. The Brahmins worship it and offer prayers to it when they make their daily ablutions. It is then that they invoke the holy rivers, among others the Ganges, and all its sacred branches. Often too they offer oblations to water by casting into the rivers and tanks, especially at the places where they bathe, small pieces of gold and silver, and sometimes pearls and other valuable jewels.

Furthermore, sailors, fishermen, and all who frequent the sea, visit the shore from time to time to pay their worship and to offer up their sacrifices to it.

When after a long drought, an abundant rain brings hope to the despairing husbandman by filling the great reservoirs for the irrigation of the rice-fields, the inhabitants at once flock to them and with signs of joy exclaim, 'The goddess has arrived'; and they bow with their hands clasped towards the water which fills the reservoirs, while he-goats or rams are sacrificed in its honour.

At the season of the year when the Cauvery inundates the barren and scorched fields on

its banks and spreads freshness and fertility far and wide—which generally takes place in the middle of July—the inhabitants of that part of the Peninsula crowd to its banks, many of them coming from a great distance, in order to congratulate the lady, the water, on her arrival and to offer her sacrifies of all sorts, such as pieces of money, which they throw to her that she may have something to defray her expenses; pieces of linen to clothe herself; jewels to adorn herself; rice, cakes, fruits, and other eatables, lest she should suffer from hunger; household utensils such as baskets, earthen vessels, etc., in order that she may conveniently cook and store her provisions and have everything which may procure her an easy subsistence.

The homage which the Brahmins in the Sandhya ceremonies pay to the water contained in the copper vessel, the frequent performance of Achamana or purification by water, and many other similar acts, attest the reality of the special worship which they pay to water. Hence no doubt arises the great veneration which they have for Vishnu, who represents this element in the Trimurti; a veneration far superior to that which they show to Siva, the representative of fire.

As far as one can see, in ancient times the elements had temples specially dedicated to their worship; but I confess that I have not been able to discover any vestiges of such buildings still remaining. Nevertheless, if we may believe the evidence of a Brahmin who was consulted

on the subject by Abraham Rogers, there was, when this traveller visited India, in a district not far from the Coromandel Coast, a temple dedicated to the five elements. Be this as it may, however, one may not unfrequently see upon the door or in the interior of the temples existing at the present day the symbols of these elements represented either by five lingams arranged in a line, or by only three which are symbols of the material Trimurti—earth, water, and fire.

It may be remarked, perhaps, that the Hindus are not the only ancient nation which have adored the elements without attaching to the worship the idea of the divinities who subsequently became identified with it. Most idolatrous nations have, I am quite aware, made the elements the actual objects of their worship. But this confirms rather than contradicts the opinion that the Hindus gave themselves up to this material idolatry, and that they invented their Trimurti in order to perpetuate it by symbols. For I persist in my belief that the three great divinities, Brahma, Vishnu, and Siva, were originally nothing else but the three elements personified.

The Trimurti, as we have seen, signifies at the same time the three bodies and the three powers. These three bodies, symbolical of the three great agents of Nature, were at first simply allegorical, just as are most of the religious and political institutions of India. This decided

taste for allegory, which is characteristic of the founders of the Hindu religion and polity, has proved the source of many errors in the case of a people who are invariably guided simply by the impression of their senses, and who, accustomed to judge things only by their outward appearance, have taken literally that which was represented to them under symbols, and have thus come to adore the actual image itself instead of the reality.

This system of explanatory symbolism has always been, and is even now, so familiar to Hindu writers, that they often describe their three great divinities by the allegorical designations peculiar to each. We have seen, too, that they recognize in men three sorts of dispositions or qualities which they call Satva, Rajas and Tamas. Satva is the gentle and insinuating disposition; Rajas, the irascible, furious, passionate; Tamas, the dull, heavy, and lethargic.

They attribute one of these qualities to each of the divinities which compose the Trimurti. Thus Vishnu is endowed with Satva, Siva with Rajas, and Brahma with Tamas. Again, these same qualities are also applied to the three elements. The earth, like Brahma, is heavy and indifferent by nature; the water, like Vishnu, is insinuating and penetrating; the fire, like Siva, is capable of destroying everything by its violence.

The quality Tamas is so inherent in the earth that Hindu astronomers often confound the

two. Thus in a lunar eclipse, when the darkness of the earth intercepts the rays of the sun, they say that the *Tamas-bimbam*, or the disk Tamas, obscures by its shadow the disk of the moon.

The quality Rajas, characteristic of first and represented under the form of Siva, is ascribed in a special manner to that deity by the Hindu poets; and although the name of Siva, which is most commonly used, signifies joy, the deity bears many other names which seem to show that he is no other than fire personified. Such, for instance, is the name Jwala, the inflamed, under which he is well known.

I shall here relate a strange practice which seems to me to support the opinion I hold regarding the origin of the Trimurti. Sometimes during the periods of excessive heat the Hindus suppose that Siva, from whom it emanates, is more than usually inflamed. Consequently, fearing lest he should set everything on fire, they place over the head of his idol a vessel filled with water. In this vessel a little hole is pierced, so that the water may, by falling on him drop by drop, refresh him and abate the burning heat that consumes him.

The quality Satva, ascribed to Vishnu, applies also to water which penetrates and insinuates itself into the earth, rendering it fertile; for the name of Vishnu signifies one who penetrates everywhere. Appu (water) is a common enough name for this deity; but the commonest of all is Narayana, that is to say, one who moves upon the waters.

Furthermore, the idea that the three principal divinities of India are the elements personified is admitted by a great number of Vaishnavite Brahmins, and I am indebted to some of these for a portion of the arguments on which I have based my own view. They have at the same time told me that they themselves regard all that is commonly related on the Trimurti as mere fables; but as the disclosure of such a sentiment, which tends to nothing less than the undermining of one of the principal foundations of the popular religion, would stop the sources of their emoluments, and would at the same time expose them to public indignation, they are careful never to publish their private opinion on the matter.

This theory once admitted, it will be easy to find a very clear and natural meaning for certain expressions contained in the Hindu books—expressions which have led many authors to believe that the people of India possessed from the earliest times some knowledge of the Trinity. 'These three gods,' say those books, 'are but one; Siva is the heart of Vishnu, and Vishnu the heart of Brahma; it is one lamp with three lighted wicks.' At first sight these expressions would appear to indicate one god in three persons. But even granted it were true that the primitive Hindus intended to transmit to their posterity the idea of the Trinity under the form and attributes of the Trimurti, it must be confessed that the result has been a distorted presentation of this great mystery.

On the other hand, I believe there is another explanation which is more simple and more reasonable. I cannot indeed doubt that the Hindu writers, in using the expressions just quoted, and many others of the same kind, wished them to be understood to mean that the co-operation of the three elements in question was indispensable for the production and reproduction of everything that exists in nature, a co-operation so necessary that the absence of one would reduce the others to a state of complete inertness and impotence.

My readers have, no doubt, been astonished to find that air, the element which some ancient Greek philosophers considered to be the beginning and ending of everything created, has so far not figured in this discussion. As a matter of fact, the Hindus go farther than the Greeks. They recognize five elements, and the air is divided by them into ether and wind, or, properly speaking, air, which is personified under the name of Indra, the chief of the inferior deities and the king of the ethereal regions, where he dwells. The word Indra signifies the air; in his domains the winds blow according to his commands. In the Indra-purana we find these words: 'Indra is nothing else than the wind, and the wind is nothing else than Indra.' The wind by condensing the clouds produces lightning, which is the weapon of this deity. He launches it against the giants, with whom he is often at war; and he is sometimes victorious, sometimes vanquished. The clouds, whose

various forms represent the giants, sometimes stop the wind; sometimes, on the other hand, the latter disperses the clouds and rids the air of them.

This taste for allegory, which is inherent amongst all people in rudimentary stages of civilization, has become in the case of the Hindus an inexhaustible source of errors in matters of religion. In the earlier ages would he commentators, by interpreting in their own way ideas whose original meaning had become obscured by lapse of time, confused everything instead of making everything clear; and later their successors, wearied by attempts to explain what seemed to them inexplicable, stuck to the literal meaning, and thus revived the extravagant idolatry which forms the religious system of the modern Hindus.

3

The Worship of Animals

Hindu Religion and Mythology

Of all the different kinds of idolatry the worship of animals is certainly one of the lowest forms, and the one which most unmistakably reveals the weakness of human nature; for man thus shows himself incapable of recognizing in His works the great Creator of the universe. What a sad spectacle it is when man, created in God's own image, with a countenance so formed that he might always be looking heavenwards, so forgets his sublime origin as to dare to bow the knee to animals! It is almost incredible that human beings should so debase themselves.

But we must not lament over facts without inquiring into their causes. The worship of animals becomes more comprehensible when one considers the foundations on which all idolatrous religions are based; namely, self-interest and fear. In the eyes of a heathen anything that can be useful to him seems worthy of being worshipped; and this feeling

is much stronger in regard to anything that can harm him. Thus the Egyptians, though they were so highly cultivated in the arts and sciences, worshipped the bull Apis, the ibis, the crocodile, beetles, snakes, etc., on account either of the good they hoped for or of the harm they feared from them. As for the Hindus, they appear to be firmly convinced that as all living creatures are either useful or hurtful to man, it is better to worship them all, paying them more or less attention in proportion to the advantages they offer or the fear which their qualities inspire. First on their list of sacred creatures are the monkey, the bull, the bird called garuda, and snakes.

The Monkey or Hanuman

The great reverence in which the monkey is held by Hindus is no doubt due to its likeness to man, both in its outward appearance and in many of its habits. Perhaps also its thievish and destructive propensities may be partly accountable for the consideration which it enjoys. At any rate Hindu books are full of marvellous tales of monkeys. In my remarks in the chapter on Rama I have already described some of the deeds of valour wrought by this hero at the head of his army of monkeys. Indeed, the greater part of the Ramayana, the favourite epic of the Hindus, is devoted to the achievements of these valiant monkey soldiers and their illustrious general.

The cult of the monkey Hanuman extends over the whole of India. The followers of Vishnu are specially devoted to this deity, but all are ready to give him a share of their homage. Images of Hanuman are to be seen in most temples and in many public places. They are also to be found in forests and desert spots. Indeed, in those provinces where there are many followers of Vishnu, you can scarcely move a yard without coming across an image of this beloved god. The offerings made to him are solely of natural products, never of a sacrifice of blood. Wherever monkeys are to be found in a wild state, their devotees daily bring them offerings of boiled rice, fruit, and various other kinds of food to which they are partial. This is considered a most meritorious act.

The Bull

This is the favourite deity of the Saivaites, or followers of Siva. Many conjectures have been offered as to the origin of bull-worship among so many idolatrous peoples. It seems to me, however, that the reason is simple enough. Was it not most natural that those who worshipped so many different objects should offer homage to animals which were so pre-eminently valuable to them, which were their companions in labour, on which they relied to carry on all their agricultural work, which in primitive times constituted their one source of wealth, and which even at the present day

form the basis of material wealth all over the world?

The nations which did not actually worship them as gods were always careful to show the high value they set upon them. For instance, amongst the Romans to kill a bull was accounted as a less crime than to kill a fellow-citizen; and it was along time before the Athenians could bring themselves to offer up one of these animals in their sacrifices. There is, every reason therefore why the Hindus should regard their cattle with extraordinary veneration, for as a matter of fact oxen and cows are so absolutely necessary to them that one may safely say it would be quite impossible for them to exist without their help. For this reason, therefore, these animals are reckoned among the most sacred objects of their religion. Their images are to be found in almost every temple, particularly in those dedicated to Siva, and are to be seen in great numbers in those districts where the sect of the Lingayats predominates. The sacred bull is usually represented as lying down on a pedestal, with three of his legs doubled under him, and the right forefoot extended straight out beyond his head[1].

Live bulls are also regarded as objects of public worship by Hindu devotees. By way of investing them with an appearance of sanctity

1. There is an enormous specimen in Tanjore temple.

these sacred beasts are branded on the right hind quarter with a design representing Siva's special weapon. They are allowed perfect liberty, are never tied up in a shed, and may graze wherever they please. They are often to be seen in the streets, where their devotees worship them publicly and at the same time bring them rice and different kinds of grain to eat. They are all under the safeguard of superstition, and though they wander hither and thither night and day, I have never heard of one being stolen. When they die, even the Pariahs dare not eat their flesh, the bodies being buried with much pomp and ceremony.

Priests of Siva sometimes travel from district to district with these sacred bulls, whose horns and bodies are decorated with much taste. Large crowds accompany them, carrying flags of various colours and headed by bands of music. The real object of all this display is to collect alms from the faithful, an object which is invariably attained; for multitudes flock to worship the venerated animal, prostrating themselves before it with every demonstration of devotion that superstition can suggest, and one and all never forget to recompense the leader of the procession, who, when he thinks that he has collected sufficient contributions, sets the sacred beast at liberty again.

Garuda

The kite garuda is held in great honour, especially by the followers of Vishnu.

Brahmins, after finishing their morning ablutions, will wait till they have seen one of these birds before returning to their homes. They call this a lucky meeting, and go back fully convinced that it will bring them good luck for the rest of the day. It is a common bird enough. Naturalists classify it among the eagles (the Malabar eagle), but it is the smallest of the species. It measures barely a foot from its beak to the tip of its tail, and about two feet and a half across its outspread wings. Its body is covered with glossy feathers of a bright chestnut colour; its head, neck, and breast are whitish; the ends of its wings are a glossy black; its feet are yellow, with black claws. It is a pretty and graceful bird to look at; but its offensive odour renders a near acquaintance unpleasant. It utters a harsh, shrill, quavering cry like *kra! kra!* the last note of which is prolonged into a mournful wail. Though apparently strong and vigorous, it never attacks any bird larger than itself that would be likely to offer resistance.

Indeed its timid and cowardly nature makes one doubt whether it really does belong to the same species as the king of the featured tribe. It wages perpetual war upon lizards, rats, and especially snakes. When it espies one of the last named, it swoops down upon it, seizes it in its talons, carries it up an enormous height, and then lets it drop. Following swiftly, it picks it up again, killed of course by its fall, and flies off with it to some neighbouring tree where it may be devoured at leisure. Probably out of

gratitude for the services tendered by this bird in ridding the country of reptiles, the Hindus have erected shrines in its honour, just as the Egyptians, from a similar motive, placed the ibis amongst their tutelary deities.

The garuda also feeds on frogs and any small fish that it can seize in shallow water. Moreover, it does not show much consideration for the poultry-yards of its woshippers, on which it often makes a raid. But its cowardice is such that an angry hen defending her chickens can easily put it to flight, and only the chickens which have imprudently wandered from their mother's side are likely to fall into its clutches. Protected by superstition, the bird has no fear of man; it may often be seen on the roof of a house, or in some frequented place. Sunday is the day specially devoted to garuda-worship. I have often seen Vaishnavites assembled together on that day for the express purpose of paying it homage. They call the birds around them by throwing pieces of meat into the air, which the birds catch very cleverly with their claws.

To kill one of these birds would be considered as heinous a crime as homicide, especially in the eyes of the followers of Vishnu. If they come across one that has been accidentally killed, they give it a splendid funeral. And they pay the same respect to the dead remains of a monkey or a snake, performing in each case various ceremonies, in order to expiate the wickedness of the unknown author of this dreadful crime.

Snakes

Among the many dangerous animals which infest India, snakes are certainly the most to be dreaded. Though tigers are no doubt very formidable enemies, they are not answerable for nearly so many deaths as snakes. During my stay in India hardly a month passed without my hearing that some person has been killed, close to where I happened to be living, by the bite of a poisonous snake. One of the commonest snakes, and at the same time the most venomous, is the cobra, the bite of which causes almost immediate death. It is, accordingly held, in peculiar veneration.

Snake-worship, which is a common form of idolatry among almost every heathen nation, no doubt owes its origin to men's natural fear of these reptiles. They try to propitiate the poisonous species with offerings and sacrifices, and they treat those which do not possess deadly fangs with the same amount of respect, because in their ignorance they attribute to a benevolent instinct what is really only due to want of power.

As if the actual presence of these dangerous reptiles were not sufficient to terrify the native mind, Hindu books are filled with stories and fables about them, and pictures or images of them meet you at every turn.

Snake-worshippers search for the holes where they are likely to be found, and which

more often than not are in the little mounds raised by the kariahs, or white ants. When they have found one, they visit it from time to time, placing before it milk, bananas, and other food which the snake is likely to fancy. If a snake happens to get into a house, far from turning out the inconvenient guest and killing it on the spot, they feed it plentifully and offer sacrifices to it daily. Hindus have been known to keep deadly snakes for years in their houses, feeding and petting them. Even if a whole family were in danger of losing their lives, no one member of it would be bold enough to lay sacrilegious hands on such an honoured inmate.

Temples have also been erected in their special honour. There is a particularly famous one in eastern Mysore, at a place called Subramaniah, which is also the name of the great snake so often mentioned in Hindu fable[1]. Every year in the month of December a solemn feast is held in this temple. Innumerable devotees flock to the sacred spot from all parts to worship and offer sacrifices to the snakes. An enormous number of the reptiles have taken up their abode inside the building, where they are fed and looked after by the officiating Brahmins. The special protection thus afforded has allowed them to increase to such an extent that they may be met with at every turn all over the

1. It is also called Ananta and Mahasesha. It is on this snake that Vishnu reclines while sleeping on the sea.

neighbourhood. Many of their worshippers take the trouble to bring them food. And woe to him who should have the audacity to kill one of these gruesome deities. He would get himself into terrible trouble[2].

Fish

The denizens of water also come in for their share of Hindu worship. It is quite a common thing to see Brahmins throwing rice or other food to the fishes in rivers and tanks. Where the Brahmins exercise undisputed authority, fishing is strictly prohibited, as, for instance, near the large Agraharas, or Brahmin villages; and in those parts of the rivers where they are in the habit of bathing I have often seen huge shoals of large fish swimming about near the surface, waiting for their food. At the slightest sound they will rush in hundreds towards the bank, and they are so tame that they will actually feed out of a man's hand.[3]

What I have said so far gives but a feeble notion of the superstitious feelings with which Hindus regard animals. Ought these feelings, as some writers think, to be attributed to their extreme tender-heartedness, to their gentle and compassionate natures? I should say decidedly not. Such childish, yet shameful, forgetfulness of the superiority of man over all other created beings cannot surely arise from any noble

---

2. There are many temples of this description still existing, to which pilgrimages are made.

3. Fish-worship is connected with the fish avatar.

sentiments. I only see in it the foolish errors of a weak-minded people, who are slaves to the idle fancies of their own imaginations, and whose reason has become so obscured that they are incapable of recognizing the dust and natural laws governing the life of mankind. The most irreconcilable superstition and the most ill-conceived considerations of self-interest are the only motives which actuate Hindus in this idolatry of birds and beasts. Anyone who has made a careful study of the character of Brahmins, who display so much care and tenderness for monkeys, snakes, and birds of prey, will soon perceive that these same men show the most utter callousness and indifference for the misfortunes and wants of their fellow-men.

Bhootas, or Evil Spirits

Almost all ancient philosophers, among them Pythagoras and the followers of Plato, have agreed in saying that each human being is under the influence of a good spirit or an evil spirit; some even go so far as to allow him both a good and a bad spirit. Our own revealed religion can suggest more reasonable ideas on this subject; but superstition, the creature of ignorance and fear, was obliged to fall back on the imagination to find plausible reasons for the alternations of good and evil to which mankind is subject. Incapable of a just appreciation of the workings of Providence,

and unable to fathom that which is inscrutable, these heathen people imagine that the sorrows and troubles which befall them are all the work of invisible and malicious spirits, to whom they must offer prayers and sacrifices by way of propitiation. Hindus carry their credulity on this point to a ridiculous excess. The worship of evil spirits is in fact firmly established and very generally practised among them. These spirits are called by the generic name of Bhootas, which also means elements, as if the elements were nothing else but evil spirits materialized and were the primary cause of all natural disturbances and troubles. Such demons are also called pisachas, dehias, etc.

There are temples specially dedicated to the worship of evil spirits; and there are some districts where this particular form of idolatry holds almost exclusive sway. Most of the inhabitants of the long range of hills which bounds Mysore on the west acknowledge no other deity than the devil. Each family has its own bhootas, to which it offers daily prayers and sacrifices in order that he may preserve its members from the ills which the bhootas of their enemies might bring upon them. Bhoota images are to be found all over these hills. Sometimes they are idols with hideous faces, but more often they are merely shapeless blackened stones. Every bhoota has its own particular name. Some are thought to be more

powerful and more spiteful than others and these are naturally most widely worshipped.[1]

All these evil spirits delight in sacrifices of blood. Buffaloes, pigs, goats, cocks, and other living animals are frequently slain in their honour; and when rice is offered to them it must be dyed with blood. They do not disdain to accept offerings of intoxicating liquors and drugs, or even flowers, provided they are red.

I have noticed that the worship of evil spirits is most prevalent in mountainous regions and in sparsely populated rural tracts. The inhabitants of these out-of-the-way districts have little communication with more civilized parts, and are more ignorant, more cowardly, and consequently more superstitious even than their more civilized fellow-countrymen. All the troubles and misfortunes that happen to them are put down to their bhootas, whose anger they think they have somehow incurred; and it is for the purpose of disarming this malevolence that they are so prodigal in their worship of them.

The wild tribes scattered through the forests of Malabar, on the Carnatic Hills, and elsewhere, where they are known as Kadu-

1. The system of demon-worship seems to have been that of the tribes whom the Hindus supplanted and drove into the mountains or into the extreme south. The Brahmins have given a place to those demons in their system, and represent them as attendants of Siva (Bhutesa = lord of demons).

Kurumbars, Sholigars, Irulers, etc., worship no other gods but these bhootas.

Sacrifices

In vain has the attempt been made, for the credit of humanity, to throw doubt upon the many evidences of human sacrifices; but unfortunately, the proofs are too strong; they are written in blood in the history of many nations, and can be only too clearly proved. Man, overwhelmed with infirmities and misfortunes, and fully convinced that they were the punishment of his sins, imagined that he would appease and propitiate the gods by offering them the noblest and most perfect sacrifice that he could find. Firmly imbued with this horrible idea, he considered himself justified in shedding the blood of human victims as well as that of animals. If such an atrocious custom needed confirmation, recent instances of it could be quoted among the Hindus, who, in common with other heathen nations, have not scrupled to drench the altars of their gods with the blood of their fellow-men.

I will say nothing of the abominable teachings of their magicians in this respect. Criminal abuses committed by a few are no proof of the absence of religion and morality in a nation as a whole. If an infamous charlatan ventures to assure powerful patrons who are

so weak as to have recourse to his arts, that it is necessary to shed human blood in order to ensure success in his mysterious operations, and if it is only too certain that unfortunate virgins have been sacrificed at the saktis of these magicians, the disgrace of it all must rest on the heads of those who are responsible for the maintenance of social order.

A similar sacrifice, however, is recommended when the grand yajna is performed; and though a horse is most often offered, still the Nara-medha, or sacrifice of a human victim, is held to be infinitely more pleasing to the deity who is the object of the ceremony; and is consequently to be preferred. There is, furthermore, not a single province in India where the inhabitants do not still point out to the traveller places where their Rajahs used to offer up to their idols unfortunate prisoners captured in war. These horrible sacrifices were performed with a view to securing success to their campaigns through the intervention of the gods. I have visited several places where these scenes of carnage used to be enacted. They are generally situated on the top of a mountain or in some isolated spot; and there you find a mean-looking temple, or sometimes only a little shrine containing the idol in whose honour all this human blood was spilt. The victims were beheaded, and their heads were then hung up as trophies before the bloodthirsty deity. Sometimes the sacrificers contented

themselves with cutting off the nose and ears of a prisoner; a very common form of punishment in India, and then sent him away thus mutilated. A little pagoda still exists, perched on the mountain at the foot of which lies the town of Mysore, not far from Seringapattam, which enjoyed a wide notoriety owing to the number of executions which took place there when heathen princes still ruled the country.[1]

Old men have told me that this horrible custom was still practised when they were young. There was nothing in it, according to their views, contrary to law or to the rights of the people as understood by the then reigning princes. It was based on the principle that reprisals were fair and legitimate in war; and it was accepted by the people without any feeling of horror. If fact, the old men spoke of it with the utmost as if it were the most natural thing in the world.

It is, I fear, indisputable that human sacrifices have been offered, both in ancient and modern times, on the altars of Hindu divinities. If any additional proof be needed it may be found in the Kali-purana. Abominable rites of this kind are there expressly enjoined. The ceremonies which should accompany

1. In the Aztec, Toltec, Mayan cultures of S. America, the best human beings were sacrificed every day, because they thought that otherwise the sun will not rise; and in China the rulers sacrificed most of their prisoners in their temples whenever they had them.

—Ed.

them are described in the minutest detail, as also the results which will ensue. The same book contains rules of procedure in sacrificing animals, and mentions the kinds and qualities of those which are suitable as victims. Lastly, it specifies those deities to whom these bloody offerings are acceptable. Among them are Bhairava, Yama, Nandi, and, above all, the bloodthirsty goddess Kali.

To offer human sacrifices is regarded as the exclusive right of princes, and they are even enjoined to offer them. Neither a Brahmin nor a Kshatriya may ever be sacrificed. Every human victim must be free from all bodily blemish, and must not have been guilty of any serious crime. All animals that are offered as sacrifices must be at least three years old, and must be healthy and free from all defects. Under no circumstances can Brahmins preside or assist in any way at a sacrifice of blood.

4

Inanimate Gods of Worship

Voltaire thought it incredible that the Egyptians could ever have worshipped onions and, other products of hillier gardens. He always jeered at this tradition, and looked upon it as a mere fable. But the fact is, in matters of superstition, truth is sometimes stranger than fiction. What I have already said and what I am now about to say respecting the Hindus will show incontestably that there are absolutely no limits to idolatry. The Brahmins, indeed, must needs borrow objects from all three kingdoms of nature in order to arrive at the magnificent total of three hundred and thirty millions of deities which they recognize[1]. Amongst the inanimate substances which they worship, there are four which they consider especially sacred, namely, the Salagrama stone, Darbha grass, the plant Tulasi, and the Aswattha or sacred fig-tree.

1. These are properly speaking devas or divine beings. not deities in the strict sense of the term.

The Salagrama[2]

This little stone is held in great honour throughout India. Brahmins consider it to be a metamorphosis of Vishnu, and for this reason they offer daily sacrifices to it. It is a sort of fossilized shell, ammonite or nautilus, oval, striated, umbilicated, and ornamented with 'arborizations' or tree-like markings on the outside. The more there are of these tree-like markings, the more highly they are revered.

It is obligatory for every Brahmin to have one of these stones in his possession. They are handed down from father to son, and are regarded as precious heirlooms which must never pass out of the family. It is written in the Atharva-Veda that any Brahmin's house in which there is no Salagrama is to be considered as impure as a cemetery, and the food which is prepared in it as unclean as a dog's vomit.

Though the Salagrama is looked upon as one of the metamorphoses of Vishnu, it partakes at the same time of the essence of all the other deities, and through it puja can be offered to all of them. There is nothing more efficacious for the remission of sins, no matter how grievous they may be, than to possess some water in which the Salagrama has been washed. Forgiveness of sins may even be obtained by simply touching the water which

—

2. The Salagrama or ammonite found in the Gandak and other rivers flowing through Nepal is said to be a form of Vishnu.—Pope.

has been thus sanctified. He who always keeps such water in his house ensures thereby perpetual wealth; and if he goes further and drinks it, he will not only obtain forgiveness of his sins, but he will also secure his happiness in this world, will always do what is right, and after death will at once enjoy the delights of Swarga. But before drinking this marvellous water he must not forget to address the following prayer ro Vishnu: 'Narayana, you are the ruler of the world; it is your pleasure to confer blessings on all created beings. I drink this water in which your sacred feet have been washed; I drink it that I may be cleansed from my sins; vouchsafe to pardon me, who am the greatest of sinners.'

The Tulasi

The Tulasi (Ocymum sanctum) plant is to be found everywhere in sandy and uncultivated places. It is a species resembling the basil that grows in Europe. Brahmins consider it to be the wife of Vishnu, and revere it accordingly. 'Nothing on earth can equal the virtues of the Tulasi,' say they: *Tulasi-tulana-nasti, ataeva Tulasi.* Puja must be offered daily to it. When a Brahmin is dying one of these plants is fetched and placed on a pedestal. After puja has been offered to it a bit of its root is placed in the mouth of the dying man, and the leaves are placed on his face, eyes, ears, and chest; he is then sprinkled from head to foot with a tulasi twig which has been dipped in water. While this ceremony is being performed his friends

cry several times aloud, Tulasi! Tulasi! Tulasi! The man can then die in the happy certainty that he will go straight to Swarga[1].

To obtain pardon of all one's sins it is sufficient to look at this sacred plant. By touching it a man is purified from all defilement, and if he performs the namaskara to it, any illness from which he may be suffering will be cured.

Salvation is assured to anyone who waters and attends to it every day. If a branch of it is offered to Vishnu in the month of Kartika, it will be more pleasing to the god than a thousand cows. Whoever offers to Vishnu at any time whatsoever, a spray of Tulasi that has been dipped in saffron, is assured of becoming like Vishnu himself, and of enjoying a share in Vishnu's happiness. To give a twig of Tulasi to anyone who is in any danger, or who is suffering from anxieties and cares, is a certain means of securing for him a satisfactory ending to his difficulties.

These are only a few of the many virtues possessed by the Tulasi.

Most Brahmins cultivate the plant in their houses, and offer it daily prayers and sacrifices. They also take care that it shall grow near the places where they perform their ablutions, and in their meeting-places, such as the chattras. The Tulasi is usually planted on a little mound of sand, which they call Brindavanam[2], or on a square pillar, three or four feet In height,

1. This formality is observed only by the Vishnavites.

— H.B.

2. This name is also given to the place inhabited by Krishna.

hollow at the top, with its four sides facing the four points of the compass. Brahmins consider it a peculiarly meritorious act to carefully water and cultivate the plant[1].

Its leaves have a sweet aromatic scent and act as a cough elixir and cordial; indeed Hindus think that they possess many medicinal properties. Brahmins always swallow one or two after their meals, as an aid to digestion. They also eat some both before and after performing their ablutions in cold water, in order to keep up the proper temperature in the stomach and to prevent colds and chills and other maladies which might attack them without this preventive. It was probably in consequence of its medicinal properties that the Hindus deified the plant in the first instance.

Darbha Grass[2]

This plant belongs to the genus borage. It is found everywhere, especially in damp marshy ground. Brahmins always keep some in their houses, and it is used in all their ceremonies. It grows to the height of about two feet and is finely pointed at the top. It is extremely rough to the touch, and if rubbed the wrong way it cuts through the skin and draws blood.

---

1. The plant is grown in the courtyard of almost every Brahmin house, and the women offer worship to it daily.—H.B.

2 This sacred grass (Poa cynosuroides) is essential in all sacrifices.—H.B.

Hindu legends differ as to the origin of this sacred grass. Some say that it was produced at the time when the gods and the giants were all busy churning, with the mountain Mandara, the sea of milk in order to extract from it amrita or nectar, which would render them all immortal. The story is that the mountain, while rolling about on Vishnu's back (who, under the form of a turtle, was supporting it) rubbed off a great many of the god's hairs, and that these hairs, cast ashore by the waves, took root there and became Darbha grass.

Others say that the gods, while greedily drinking the amrita which they had with infinite pains extracted from the sea of milk, let fall a few drops of the nectar on this grass, which thus became sacred. Then, again, others assert that it was produced at the time when Mohini—that is to say, Vishnu metamorphosed into a courtesan of that name—was distributing amrita to the gods. The vessel containing the nectar was supported on Mohini's hip, from which some fleshy filaments fell, and taking root in the ground, developed under the form of Darbha grass.

Be this as it may, Darbha grass is looked upon as part of Vishnu himself. On the strength of this the Brahmins worship it and offer sacrifices to it, and, as may be remembered, make use of it in all their ceremonies, in the belief that it possesses the virtue of purifying everything. An annual feast instituted in honour of the sacred Darbha grass is celebrated on the eighth day of the moon in the month of Bhadra, and is called the Darbha-ashtami. By

offering the grass as a sacrifice on that day immortality and blessedness for ten ancestors may be secured; and another result is that one's posterity increases and multiplies like the Darbha grass itself, which is one of the most prolific members of the vegetable kingdom. I have no idea why this plant should have been selected as worthy of special honour. I have never heard of its being endowed with any peculiar properties, either medicinal, culinary, or other, which would account for its high position.

The Sacred Fig Tree

There are seven different species of trees which the Brahmins consider sacred and accordingly worship; but, strange to say, they are not those which produce the best fruits. It is true, however, that their thick foliage makes a splendid shade—a priceless boon in the hot climate of India. The Aswattha[1] comes first on the list. It is one of the most beautiful trees in the country, and grows to a huge size. It is to be found everywhere, but especially where the Brahmins perform their ablutions. Its large leaves, very soft to the touch, in colour bright green, are so light and thin that the slightest breeze sets them in motion; and as they produce an impression of most refreshing coolness, the tree is considered to possess health-giving properties.

1. It is called Arasa-maram in Tamil; Ravi-manu in Telugu; Arulimara in Canarese. It is the pagoda fig tree (Ficus-religiosa), the tree of God.

When stirred by a breeze the leaves make a pleasant rustle, which Hindu authors have sometimes likened to the melodious sounds of the vina. When to all these attractive natural characteristics is added the tradition that under this tree Vishnu was born, it is no wonder that the Aswattha is regarded with great respect and veneration. No one is allowed to cut it down, lop off its branches, or even pull off its leaves unless they are to be used for acts of worship. To fell one of these trees would be an awful sacrilege, and quite unpardonable. It is consecrated to Vishnu, or rather it is Vishnu himself under the form of a tree[1]. Sometimes a solemn inaugural ceremony is gone through, called Aswattha-pratistha, or the consecration of the Aswattha tree. This ceremony, which is an elaborate and costly one, possesses the virtue of transforming the tree into a divinity by inducting Vishnu into it. The Brahmins assert that untold blessings will be showered upon anyone who is willing to bear the expense.

Sometimes it is invested, like a Brahmin, with the triple cord, the very same ceremonies being performed. And sometimes it is solemnly married. Generally a Vepu or margosa tree[2] is

1 The Aswattha or Pipal, having roots hanging from above and branches bent downwards, is allegorical. Each tree springing from an unperceived root is emblematical of the body. which really springs from and is one with the Godhead. In the Bhagavat-gita it is said to typify the universe. It is said to be the male of the Vata or banian (Ficus indica).—Ed.

2. This is another sacred tree, which is dedicated to Siva.

selected for its spouce, and occasionally a plantain or banana tree. Almost the same formalities are observed for this curious marriage as in the case of a marriage between Brahmins. Here and there, on the high-roads and elsewhere, the Aswattha and Vepu trees may be seen planted side by side on little mounds. This union is not an accidental one, but the result of an actual marriage ceremony. Not thirty yards from the modest hut where I wrote these pages were two of these trees, under whose shade I have often reclined. Their trunks were so closely entwined that they had become incorporated one with another. The inhabitants of the village could remember to have seen them planted together some fifty years before, and said that they had been present at the wedding festivities, which lasted several days, and were celebrated at the expense of a wealthy person of the neighbourhood at a cost of more than 1,500 rupees.

Such, then, are the kind of good works which Hindus perform in order to obtain the pardon of their sins in this world and to ensure their happiness in the next.

5

The Doctrine of Metempsychosis

There are few Hindu books in which the doctrine of metempsychosis, or Punarjanma, is not explained and expounded. This doctrine is, as is generally known, one of the fundamental principles of the Hindu religion. The following is an extract from the Bhagavata:

'Vishnu, the Supreme Being, before he created anything which now exists, began by creating souls, which at first animated bodies of fantastic shapes. During their union with these bodies they either committed sin or practised virtue. After a long abode in these provisional dwelling-places, they were withdrawn and summoned before the tribunal of Yama, who judges the dead. This divinity admitted into Swarga (paradise) those souls which had led virtuous lives; and he shut up in Naraka (hell) those souls, which had given themselves up to sin. Souls which had been partly virtuous and partly sinful were sent to earth to animate other bodies, and so to endure proportionately the pain due for their sins and to receive the reward of their virtues.

Thus every new birth, whether happy or unhappy, is the result of deeds practised in previous generations, and is either the reward or punishment for them.[1] We may thus judge by the condition of a person in an existing generation what he has been in the previous one.

'Nevertheless, those who die in holiness are no longer exposed to new births; they go straight to Swarga.

'The souls of men, after death, go to animate other bodies. Sometimes it is the body of an insect, of a reptile, of a bird, or of a quadruped, and sometimes it is the body of another man. Nevertheless, the most perfect are admitted into Swarga, and the most guilty are plunged into Naraka. It is solely according to their good or bad deeds that their transmigration, advantageous or otherwise, is determined; and the good or evil they will have to experience in the various states through which they pass is determined in the same manner.

'The distinctions and differences which are to be observed amongst mankind must be attributed to the same causes. Some are rich,

1. The philosophers of the School of Pythagoras held that these souls were not only immortal but eternal; that is to say, they existed before they entered the bodies of living creatures. The soul, they said, cannot be born of anything mortal; otherwise all things might become immortal. Nor can the soul be reborn of anything immortal, because that which is immortal cannot be reproduced. They held, therefore, that the soul is part of God Himself.

and others poor; some are weakly, others enjoy good health; some are handsome, others ugly; some are of low birth, others highly born; some are happy, others unhappy. These differences are not the result of mere chance, but of goodness or wickedness, as the case may be, in preceding existences.

'Man is the highest form of all the creatures on earth. To be born a man, in whatever caste it may be, always presupposes a certain degree of merit.

'Among men the Brahmins hold the first rank. The honour of giving a soul to a Brahmin is the reward only of the accumulated merits of many previous generations.

'To practise virtue in the hope of some reward is always a good thing; but to practise it with entire disinterestedness and without expecting any return or recompense, this is the most perfect. Those who thus practise it are certain of the happiness of Swarga, and are no more subject to change.

'This then is the fruit of our deeds. This is the reason why the same soul lives sometimes in the body of a man, at other times in that of an animal. This is why it is at one time happy, at another time unhappy in this world and in the other.'

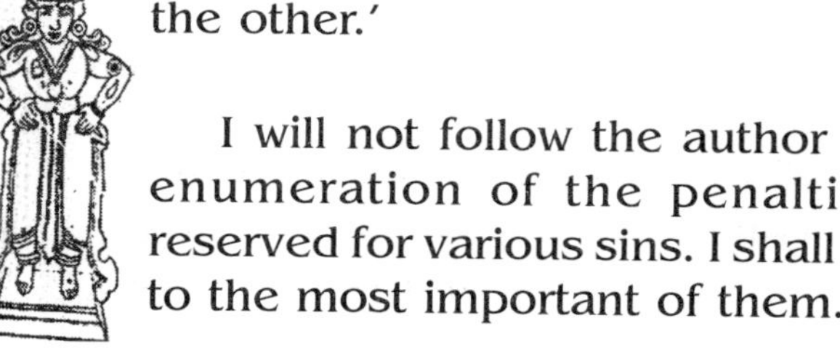

I will not follow the author in his detailed enumeration of the penalties which are reserved for various sins. I shall confine myself to the most important of them.

'He who kills the cow of a Brahmin will go after death to hell, where he will for ever be the prey of serpents, and tormented by hunger and thirst. After thousands of years of horrible sufferings he will return to the world to animate the body of a cow, and will remain in this state as many years as the cow has hairs on its body. At length he will be born a Pariah, and will be afflicted with leprosy for a period of ten thousand years.

'The murder of a Brahmin, for any cause whatsoever, is a sin four times more heinous than the former. Whoever is guilty of it will be condemned at his death to take the form of one of those insects which feed on filth. Being reborn long afterwards a Pariah, he will belong to this caste, and will be blind for more than four times as many years as there are hairs on the body of a cow. He can, nevertheless, expiate his crime by feeding forty thousand Brahmins.

'If a Brahmin kills a Sudra, it willsuffice to efface the sin altogether if he recites the Gayatri a hundred times.

'He who kills an insect will himself become an insect after death. Then he will be reborn a Sudra, but, he will be subject to all sorts of infirmities.

'Every Brahmin who cooks for a Sudra or who travels mounted on an ox will go to hell after death. He will be plunged there into boiling oil and be bitten continuously by venomous snakes. He will be reborn afterwards

under the form of one of those birds of prey which devour corpses, and will remain a thousand years under this form, and also a hundred years under the form of a dog.

'Whoever fells a sacred fig-tree commits a crime four times greater than the murder of a Brahmin, and will be exposed after his death to penalties proportionate to a sin so heinous.'

Several modern philosophers have maintained that Pythagoras attached only an allegorical sense to the doctrine of metempsychosis. The most general opinion is that he taught it merely as an abstract religious doctrine. He is said to have borrowed it from the Egyptians, who, if we are to believe Herodotus, were its inventors. But **the communications between Pythagoras and the Brahmins and Gymnosophists of India lead one to suppose with quite as much reason that he borrowed it from these Indian philosophers, for we know that the Hindus have never copied anything from contemporaneous nations.** If it be true that at the time of the travels of Pythagoras the doctrine of metempsychosis was professed by the Egyptians, they had probably taken their ideas from the same sources as the people of India, if indeed they had not actually borrowed them from the latter.

It is certain, furthermore, that it is not in this alone that the metaphysics of Pythagoras

present some features of resemblance to those of the Gymnosophists. Again, we know that Pythagoras travelled for his own instruction, and it has never been contended that he taught anything to the peoples of Asia whom he visited. Besides, various Hindu books, which undoubtedly existed before the time of Pythagoras, are filled with this doctrine of metempsychosis and treat it as an article of their primitive faith, which had been well established before his time. Anyhow, whoever the originator of it may be, it is none the less wonderful that such a chimerical system was not only acknowledged in almost the whole of Asia, but has even found credence in various other parts of the world. It is well known that Caesar found it in full force amongst the Gauls; and one is astonished to find that enlightened men like Socrates and Plato made these fantastic theories the object of their serious speculations. Have we not seen modern writers, too, contending that the doctrine of metempsychosis is a masterpiece of genius? They have indeed maintained that Aristotle admitted the transmigration of the soul of one man into another, though it is proved that he rejected as absurd the Idea of the transmigration of human souls into the bodies of beasts.

In consequence of his belief Pythagoras deprecated the eating of the flesh of any living creature, lest per chance a son might feed on the body of his father and thus repeat the

horrible feast of Thyestes. The most zealous of his disciples ate only vegetables; and they even excluded beans from their meals. In the same way the Brahmins still refuse to eat onions, mushrooms, and certain other vegetables. Still, the example of these more rigorous disciples of Pythagoras found few imitators among the rest.

Either Pythagoras conceived a false impression of the motives of the abstinence which he had seen practised by the Hindus, or else he wished to excel them and to exaggerate their system according to his own manner.

As a matter of fact, everything induces us to believe that the Hindus are not so foolish as to believe, when they show repugnance to feeding on anything which has had life, that they might be swallowing the limbs of their ancestors. In proof of this I may remark that the Lingayats, that is to say, the followers of Siva, reject in total the doctrine of metempsychosis, yet they abstain from all animal food more religiously than the Brahmins themselves.

The fear of pollution and the horror of murder are in fact the principal causes of the antipathy of Hindus to this kind of food. Their primitive teachers, as I have already remarked, simply had in view, when counselling such abstinence, the preservation of useful animals, and also the preservation of health. It was superstition, impetuous as a flood, that always tended to overflow the banks of reason.

We know how susceptible and fastidious a respectable Hindu is in the matter of pollution. How then could a meat diet agree with his principles in this respect? The putrefaction of animals, which in a hot country manifests itself so quickly and in so disagreeable a manner; the comparative facility, on the other hand, with which products of the earth and other inorganic substances can be kept from the putrefying influence of the sun; the horror, so strongly felt, of feeding on the remains of a dead body; and a number of other prejudices which the leaders of the Hindu religion have been interested in fostering, are reasons sufficiently powerful to act upon minds prepared for them by custom and education. Let us add to these considerations the horror inspired by murder among Hindus in general—a horror which is so great in the case of many that it induces them to spare even the lives of filthy and troublesome insects; for the Brahmins are persuaded that there is no difference between the souls of men and those of the vilest of living things. Hence **they hold that there is, morally speaking, as much crime in crushing an ant as in committing a murder.**

The majority of the Sudras feel no scruples, it is true, in killing animals and eating their flesh, the cow alone excepted. They even include in their ranks butchers and professional hunters, such as the Boyas or Baiders who inhabit the jungles and mountains and live on the products of the chase. But it is also proper to remark that it is this violation of a respected

usage which in a great measure brings upon them the contempt of the higher castes.

At first the doctrine of metempsychosis appears to have been limited to the successive transmigrations of souls into various human bodies. Later on, however, it received a new expansion, that the souls could migrate to the bodies of beasts and to all material objects. The Platonic philosophers, who were ridiculed for assuming that the soul of a king might enter the body of a monkey, or that of a queen the body of a grasshopper, tried to evade the difficulty by reducing the doctrine to its primitive simplicity, that is to say, by limiting the transmigration of the souls of men to human bodies and those of beasts to their own species. Plotinus and Porphyry even ventured to assert that it was thus that their master had intended it to be understood. But their retraction was too late. It is always a mistake to endeavour to restore a building which is not solid in its foundations. The Hindus, who are more persevering and less exposed to the contradictions of enlightened men, have religiously preserved their own doctrine of metempsychosis in all its entirety.

After all, the doctrine seems to have been invented merely to justify, under a gross allegory, the ways of the Supreme Being in the dispensation of rewards and punishments. The first doctrinal article admitted by the Hindus is common to the Pythagoreans; namely, that sin ought to be punished and virtue rewarded. This of course does not usually take place in the

present life, since very often vice is triumphant and virtue crushed. In order to remedy this the gods, who hold the destinies of men in their hands, have decreed that he who during his lifetime has been an unbeliever, a thief, a murderer, etc., shall be born again a creeping insect, a wild animal, an outcaste, blind, poor, etc.

Their notions of pollution pervade everything; so the Hindus believe that a soul after death retains some of the stains and impurities contracted in preceding generations, just as an earthen vessel retains for a long time the odour of any strong liquor which it has contained. This article of belief is illustrated by the example of a woman who had been a fish in an earlier generation, and who, though really a woman in the present, still retained, it is said, an odour which betrayed her first origin. It is necessary therefore that a long succession of generations should cleanse the soul from all the impurities which have polluted it in generations preceding—impurities which will increase indefinitely if people continue to lead dissolute lives.

When the Hindus are asked what is the limit of these transmigrations, they are unable to give any positive answer. Nevertheless, their sacred books affirm that a soul only succeeds in getting rid of continual transformations when by long penance and comemplation it has raised itself to that high degree of wisdom and perfection which identifies it with the Supreme Being, that is, with Parabrahma. Before

reaching such sublime heights, it must pass through all the trials and temptations to which human weakness has been condemned, and must acquire by its own experience a complete knowledge of good and evil. It begins its transmigrations under the form of the vilest Insects, and rises little by little to the condition of man, in which state the spark of wisdom concealed in it, after having remained stationary for millions of years, is at length developed and imperceptibly leads to that state of perfection and purity which puts an end to changeful existence.

In not assigning definite periods to each transmigration of the soul the Hindu philosophers seem to be wiser than the followers of Plato, who, with absurd presumption, have seen fit to assign fixed and definite periods—in some cases three thousand, and in others ten thousand years. Further, according to the latter, the transmigration is not left to chance; each soul has its choice of abode according to the inclinations of the man in whose body it has sojourned. Thus the soul of Agamemnon passed into the body of an eagle; that of Orpheus animated a swan; that of Ajax, a lion; that of Thersites, an ape, etc.

All this is simply ridiculous. But the stumbling block of the system is recollection of the past. Since the body is only a prison, a shell, how is it that the soul, as soon as it has quitted its abode, loses all remembrance of what has befallen it? Pythagoras, it is true, used to relate to his disciples what he had successively been since the siege of Troy. But the merest caviller among them might have offered the following objection: 'Since you so well remember what you have been before your present actual existence, why do I not remember in the same manner?' Pythagoras would no doubt have, answered just as the Hindus answer, that the gift of remembrance is granted only to certain privileged souls, and that they obtain it by reciting certain appropriate mantras. Unfortunately, these mantras are not unlike the waters of the Fountain of Youth, of which everyone boasts to be the owner, but the whereabouts of which nobody knows. Plato, who was too enlightened not to recognize this weak side of the system, invented the river Lathe. The souls were obliged to drink its waters before returning to the world, and thereby entirely forget the past. The invention of this fiction required neither ingenuity nor wit. The Hindus cut the knot more freely. They say that the act of regeneration suffices to make one forget all that has been seen or done before. A child under two or three years of age does not remember one day what he did the day before; still more therefore will he forget what he was and what he did before his new birth.

This explanation is at least more simple than that of Plato, if it is not equally ingenious.

Naraka or Hell

Through the tissue of fancies which the Hindus have woven over their system of

metempsychosis, ostensibly to explain it but in practice to obscure it, we may catch a few faint gleams of the true religion, the principles of which were inculcated by the patriarchs of old. Apart from the rewards and punishments which they regard as the due retribution in this world of the good or evil which a man has done in a preceding generation, it is certain that they acknowledge a future life, and a Supreme Being, who is the rewarder of the good and the terror of the wicked. In a word, they recognize a paradise and a hell.

The Hindus agree that a place of punishment is set apart for those souls which have given themselves up entirely to sin during their life on earth. This they call Naraka or Patala. It is divided into seven principal sections, destined to contain the different kinds of sinful souls; and here they undergo torments more or less severe, according to the gravity of their crimes.

Yama, the judge of the dead, is the king of hell. He has servants to carry out his decrees, who are charged with tormenting the inhabitants of Naraka. His emissaries are constantly on the watch throughout the world. They await the moment of death, and then arrest the dead and bring them before Yama's tribunal Yama consults his records, kept by many scribes working under his orders, and containing an exact account of all the good and evil which is done on earth. According to the report submitted to him, this sovereign judge pronounces the fate of the souls which

appear before him for judgement, and awards punishments proportionate to their guilt.

Yama, however, is not the only deity possessing agents on earth for seizing upon the souls of the dead. Vishnu and Siva have also their agents, who know perfectly well the devotees of their respective patrons. When such souls die the emissaries of the two gods contend for them with Yama, and the result is a keen conflict and often a bloody battle. The special devotion to Siva or to Vishnu, however lukewarm it may have been, possesses so much merit that the emissaries of the two gods usually gain the victory over those of Yama.

As for the torments of Naraka, the punishments which the wicked have to endure there are truly terrible. I will here give an abstract of what the Padma-purana says of it:

'They are buried there in eternal darkness: only groans and frightful lamentations are heard; the sharpest pains that steel and fire can cause are inflicted without respite. There are punishments fitted to each kind of sin, to each sense, to each member of the body. Fire, steel, serpents, venomous insects, savage beasts, birds of prey, gall, poison, stenches; in a word, everything possible is employed to torment the damned. Some have a cord run through their nostrils, by which they are for ever dragged over the edges of extremely sharp knives; others are; condemned to pass through the eye of a needle; others are placed between two flat rocks, which meet, and crush without

killing them; others have their eyes pecked incessantly by famished vultures; while millions of them continually swim and paddle in a pool filled with the urine of dogs or with the mucus from men's nostrils.

The dammed do not succumb under these terrible penalties, but rend the air continually with their screams and groans, which echo throughout the whole abyss of hell and add still greater horror to this frightful dwelling place.'

The pains of hell do not endure for ever; they last proportionately to the gravity of the crimes committed. The Hindu sacred writers say nothing of eternal punishment. At the end of every yuga, they say, there takes place a universal revolution—a total change in nature. When the Kali-yuga, in which we now live; has filled its allotted span, all souls will return to the divine essence from which they were originally separated, and, the world having come to an end, the sufferings of the damned will also cease.

When the souls in hell have expiated their sins, they are sent back to the earth in order to undergo new transmigrations. Their return to the world always takes place under the form of some vile animal; and proceeding from one metamorphosis to another, after millions of years they are able to acquire the degree of virtue and perfection necessary to admit of their being again united inseparably with the Supreme Being, the Universal Soul of the world.

The Abodes of Bliss

The Hindus recognize Abodes of Bliss for the souls of those who have expiated their sins by repeated transmigrations and by the practice of virtue. There are four principal abodes:

The first is Swarga, where Indra the divinity presides, and where all virtuous souls, without distinction of caste or sex, are to be found.

The second is Vaikuntha, the paradise of Vishnu, where dwell his particular followers, Brabmins and others.

The third is Kailasa, the paradise of Siva, which is reserved for the devout worshippers of the lingam.

The fourth is Satya-loka (the Place of Truth), the paradise of Brahma, where only virtuous Brahmins have the right to enter.

The pleasures enjoyed in these several abodes are all corporal and sensual.

The souls sojourning in them, having been indulged for periods of time more or less considerable according to their respective merits, are obliged to return to the earth, there to begin their transmigrations anew. This takes place until the soul is perfectly purified—a consummation, as we have seen, which is not the affair of a few days. However, with perseverance they eventually attain it. When a soul, by virtue and penances, has become as pure as gold and has freed itself entirely from the allurements of this world, it is re-united with Parabrahma, with God, with the Universal Soul, just as a drop of water returns to the sea

from whence it came. This is the Supreme Happiness, to which the Hindus give the names of Moksha (Deliverance) and Mukti (the Last End).

Thus idolatry has at least respected some of the fundamental truths graven on the hearts of men, the knowledge of which is indispensable to the stability of all civilized society. **The people of India still preserve some positive ideas of a Supreme Being, and foresee rightly enough the immortality of the soul, and the necessity and existence of another life in which the good shall be rewarded and the wicked punished.**

What other conclusion can we draw from this than that such sacred truths will never perish from off the earth? The atheist and the materialist may heap up sophistry on sophistry in order to obscure these truths and conceal them from the eyes of nations; but their efforts are in vain. Graven on the hearts of men in indelible characters by the hand of the Almighty Himself, these truths must continue to grow and to bear fruit so long as there are reasonable creatures and civilized peoples in the world.

6

The Jain Religion

The word 'Jain' is a compound word denoting a person who has overcome human infirmities and passions. A true Jain should entirely renounce all thoughts of self. He should rise superior to the scorn or opposition to which he may be subjected on account of his religion, the principles of which he must preserve and guard unaltered even to death, being fully persuaded that it is the one and only true religion on earth, that is, the true primitive religion which was give to all mankind.

Jainism presenls resemblances to both Brahminism and Buddhism, which have been summarized as follows in Elphinstone's *History of India*: 'They agree with the Buddhas in denying the existence, or at least the activity and providence of God; in believing in the eternity of matter; in the worship of deified saints; in their scrupulous care of animal life and all the precautions which it leads to; in disclaiming the divine authority of the Vedas; and in having no sacrifices and no respect for fire. They agree with the Buddhists also in

considering a state of impassive abstraction as supreme felicity, and in all the doctrines which they hold in common with the Hindus. They agree with the Hindus in other points, such as division of caste. This exists in full force in the south and west of India, and can only be said to be dormant in the north-east for, though the Jains there do not acknowledge the four classes of the Hindus, yet a Jain converted to the Hindu religion takes his place in one of the castes from which he must all along have retained the proofs of his descent, and the Jains themselves have numerous divisions of their own, the members of which are as strict in avoiding intermarriages and other intercourse as the four classes of the Hindus. Though they reject the scriptural character of the Vedas, they allow them great authority in all matters not at variance with their religion. The principal objections to them are drawn from the bloody sacrifices which they enjoin, and the loss of animal life which burnt-offerings are liable (though undesignedly) to occasion. They admit the whole of the Hindu gods, and worship some of them, though they consider them as entirely subordinate to their own saints, who are, therefore, the proper objects of adoration.'

The following is from Mr. J.A. Baines's Census Report for 1891:

'A second offshoot from the earlier Brahminism is found in the Jain, a form of belief that still subsists and flourishes in India to this day. Its origin is veiled from us, but it bears a strong family likeness to the earlier form of Buddhism, and it is a question amongst scholars whether it rose about the same time or a little earlier. At all events it seems to have been unpopular with the Buddhists, and to have diverged less from Brahmanic orthodoxy. The monastic system was not countenanced, but ritual was simplified and women were allowed to share in it. As in Buddhism, however, the larger section of the Jains decline to allow that women can attain Nirvana. The latter, however, is with them perpetual bliss, instead of complete annihilation.

'Caste amongst the Jains, is maintained, and though they have no special reservation of the priesthood to a class, there is general tendency in that direction, and in some cases Brahmins even are employed In later years. The Jains seem to have competed with the Brahmin in literature and science, so that they fell into disfavour, and would very probably have succumbed but for the advent of the Mussulman power. In the north and west of India they are still a cultivated class, most engaged in commerce, whilst in the south where they share with the Buddhists, who preceded them, the credit of forming the Canarese and Tamil literature, they are as a rule agriculturists. Except in a few of the larger cities of the north there seems to be little sectarian hostility between them and the orthodox; and in the west, where they are still closer in customs and observances, the line

of division is scarcely traceable In parts of both tracts, there is, in the present day, a tending for Jainism to regard itself as a sect of Brahminism, in spite of the non-recognition of the divine authority of the Veda. It is probable that in compliance with this tendency many have referred to their religion as Hindu of the Jain sect, so that where sect is not separately compiled, as in the imperial series of returns, the total of the Jain religion is reduced by that number.'

In the course of time, the primitive religion gradually became considerably corrupted in several essential points, and was superseded by the superstitious and detestable sophistries of Brahminism. The ancient dogmas were forgotten or put aside by the Brahmins, who invented an entirely new system of religion, in which only a shadowy resemblance can be traced to the old Hindu faith.

It is the Brahmins who invented the four Vedas and the eighteen Puranas, the Trimurti, and the fables connected with it, such as the Avatars of Vishnu, the lingam, the worship of the cow and other animals, the sacrifice of the yajnam, etc., etc. The Jains not only reject all these spurious additions, but look upon them with absolute horror.

The Brahmins introduced all these innovations very gradually. The Jains were formerly in close communion with the Brahmins both in faith and doctrine, but they opposed these changes from the very first with

all their power. Then, seeing that their remonstrances produced no effect and that these religious innovations were daily making progress among the people, they found themselves reduced at last to the sad necessity of an open rupture with the Brahmins. **The immediate cause of this rupture was the introduction of the yajna sacrifice, at which some living creature must be immolated[1].** This, they contend, is directly opposed to the most sacred and inviolable principles of the Hindu religion; which forbids the destruction of any living thing, for any reason or on any pretext whatever.

From that moment things came rapidly to a climax; and it was then that the defenders of the pure primitive religion took the name of Jain, and formed themselves into a distinct sect, composed of Brahmins, Kshatriyas, Vaisyas, and Sudras. They were the descendants of the Hindus—of all castes who originally banded themselves together to oppose the innovations of the Brahmins, and they alone have preserved the religion of their forefathers intact to the present day.

After the schism the Jains, or true believers, perpetually taunted the Brahmins with their debased religion, and what at first merely furnished subject-matter for scholastic disputes finally became the cause of long and bloody hostilities. For a long time success was on the side of the Jains, but in the end, the majority

1. It is generally a ram.

of the Kshatriyas and other castes having seceded and adopted the innovations of the Brahmins, the latter gained the ascendant and reduced their adversaries to the lowest depths of subjection.

There are very few of the Brahmin caste who hold the opinions of the Jains. There is a village, however, called Maleyur, in South Mysore, which contains between fifty and sixty families of them. They have a famous temple there, of which the guru is a Brahmin Jain. In the other more important temples of the Jains, such as those at Belgola, Madigery, and others, the gurus or priests are recruited from the Vaisyas, or merchants. The Vaisya Jains are regarded by the Brahmins of the same sect as patitas, or fallen, because they have thus usurped the priestly office, and also because they have altered the religion of the true Jains by introducing some of the innovations of their Brahmin adversaries. This divergence of opinion, however, has not led to any serious differences between them.

The Jains are divided into several sects or schools, which differ on the subject of perfect happiness, and on the means of attaining it. One of the sects, known by the name of **Swetambara** (clad in white), teaches that there is no other moksha, that is to say, no other supreme blessedness, than that which is to be obtained from sensual pleasures, particularly that which is derived from sexual intercourse with women. This sect is, it is true, not numerous.

The school of the **Jaina-bassaru** is the most numerous, and it is subdivided into several others. Its tenets differ very little from those of the Vedanta school ot Brahminism. It recognizes the different stages of meditation as taught by the latter, and enjoins very much the same means of attaining everlasting felicity, by which they understand reunion with the Godhead.

The Religious System

The Jains acknowledge one Supreme Being, to whom they give the names of Jaineswara, Paramatma; Paraparavastu, and several others expressing the infinity of his nature.

It is to this Supreme Being alone that all the prayers, and sacrifices of the true Jains are offered; and it is to him that all the marks of respect which they pay to their holy personages, known as Saloka-purushas, and to other sacred objects represented under a human form, are really addressed; for these, on attaining moksha (supreme blessedness) after death, have become united with and incorporated into the Supreme Being.

The Supreme Being is, they say, one and indivisible, is a spirit without corporal parts or limitations. His four or principal attributes are:

1. Ananta-jnanam, infinite wisdom.
2. Ananta-darsanam, infinite intuition, omniscience, and ommpresence.
3. Ananta-viryam, omnipotence.
4. Ananta-sukham, infinite blessedness.

This noble being is entirely absorbed in the contemplation of his infinite perfections, and in the uninterrupted enjoyment of the happiness which he finds in his own essence. He has nothing in common with the things of this world, and does not interfere at all in the government of this vast universe. Virtue and vice, good and evil, are indifferent to him.

Virtue being essentially right, those who practise it in this world will find their reward in another life, either by a blessed reincar-nation, or by immediate admittance to the delights of Swarga. Vice being essentially bad and wrong, those who give way to it will be punished in another world by an unhappy reincarnation. The worst offenders will go straight to Naraka after death, there to expiate their crimes. But in no case does God intervene in the distribution of punishments or rewards, or pay any attention to the good or evil by men here below.

Matter is eternal and independent of the Godhead. That which exists now has always existed and will always exist. And not only is matter eternal, but also the order and harmony which reign throughout the universe—the fixed and unchanging move-ments of the stars, the division of light from darkness, the succession and constant renewal of the seasons, the production and reproduc-tion of animal and vegetable life, the nature and properties of the elements; in fact, all things visible are eternal, and will continue to exist just as they have existed from all time.

Metempsychosis

The fundamental doctrine of the Jains is metempsychosis. Their belief in this differs in no way from that of the Brahmins. But they do not agree with the latter with regard to the four lokas or worlds. These they refuse to recognize. They also reject the three principal Abodes of Bliss—Satyaloka, Vaikuntha, and Kailasa, that is to say, the paradises of Brahma, of Vishnu, and of Siva. They recognize three worlds only, which they describe by the generic name of Jagat-triya, and which are the Urdhwa-loka or superior world, the Adha-loka or inferior world, which they also call Patala, and the Madhya-loka or middle world, that is to say, the earth where mortals dwell.

Urdhwa-loka

This world, which is also called Swarga, is the first of the Jagat-triya, and Devendra is lord of it. There are sixteen distinct abodes in it, in each of which a different degree of happiness is enjoyed in proportion to the merits of the righteous souls who are admitted. The first and highest of these habitations is the Sadhu-dharma. Only the very purest souls have access to this, and they there enjoy unbroken happiness for thirty-three thousand years. The Achuda-karpa, which is the last and lowest of the sixteen habitations, is destined for the souls of those who possess exactly the requisite amount of merit, neither more nor less, necessary to procure their admittance into the

Urddhwa-loka. They there enjoy for one thousand years the amount of happiness which is their portion. In the other intermediate habitations the degree and duration of happiness are fixed in relative proportion to the merits of those who are admitted.

Women of the rarest beauty adorn these Abodes of Bliss. The blessed, however, have no intercourse with them. The sight alone of these enchanting beauties is sufficient to intoxicate their senses and plunge them into a perpetual ecstasy that is far superior to all mere earthly pleasures. In this respect the Swarga of the Jains differs little from that of the Brahmins.

On leaving the Urddhwa-loka at the expiration of the period assigned to them, the souls of the blessed are born again upon earth and recommence the process of transmigration.

The Adha-loka

The second world of the Jagat-triya is the Adha-loka, also called Naraka, and sometimes Patala. It is the lower or inferior regions, the abode of great sinners; that is, of those whose crimes are so heinous and so manifold that they cannot be expiated by even the lowest forms of reincarnation.

The Adha-loka is divided into seven dwelling-places, in each of which the severity of the punishments is proportionate to the gravity of the offences. The least terrible is the Retna-pravai, where erring souls are tormented

for a thousand consecutive years. The torture gradu-ally increases in intensity and duration in the other abodes, until in the Maha-damai-pravai, the seventh, the punishments reach a point of awfulness which is beyond all description. It is there that the most villainous sinners are sent, and their horrible sufferings only terminate at the end of thirty-three thousand years. Women, who from their constitutional weakness are not able to endure such extremes of suffering, are never sent to this awful Maha-damai-pravai, no matter how wicked they may have been.

The Madhya-loka

The middle world, the Madhya-loka, is the third of the Jagat-triya. It is there that mortals live, and that both virtue and vice are to be found.

This world is one reju in extent, a reju being equal to the distance over which the sun travels in six months. Jambudwipa, which is the earth on which we live, occupies only a small part of the Madhya-loka. It is surrounded on all sides by a vast ocean, and in the centre of it is an immense lake excluding for a hundred thousand yojanas, or about four hundred thousand eagles. In the middle of this loke rises the famous mountain Mahameru. Jambudwipa is divided into four equal parts, which are placed at the four cardinal points of Mahameru. India is in the part called Bharata-Kshetra.

These four divisions of jambudwipa are separated from each other by six lofty

mountains, which are called Himavata, Maha-Himavata, Nishada, Nila, Arumani, Sikari, all running in the same direction from east to west, stretching across jambudwipa from one sea to the other.

These mountains are intersected by vast valleys, where the trees, shrubs, and fruits, which all grow wild, are of a beautiful pink colour. These delicious retreats are inhabited by good and virtuous people. Children of either sex living there arrive at maturity forty-eight hours after their birth. The inhabitants are not subject to pain or sickness. Always happy and contented, they live on the succulent vegetables and delicious fruits which nature produces for them without any cultivation. After death they go straight to the delights of Swarga.

A spring lies on the top of Mahameru which feeds fourteen large rivers, of which the principal are the Ganges and the Indus. All these rivers pursue a regular and even course, which never varies. Unlike the false Ganges and the false Indus of the Brahmins, the waters of which rise and fall, the Ganges and Indus of the Jains can never be forced, and their waters always maintain the same level.

The names of the fourteen rivers of the Jains are the Ganges, the Indus, the Rohita, Toya, the Rohita, the Hari-Toya, the Harikanta, the Sitta, the Sitoda, the Nan, the Narikanta, the Swarna-kula, the Rupaya-kula, the Rikta, and the Riktoda.

The sea which surrounds Jambudwipa is two hundred thousand yojanas, or eight hundred thousand miles long.

Beyond this ocean there are three other continents, separated from each other by an immense sea. They closely resemble Jambudwipa, and are also inhabited by human beings.

At the far end of the fourth continent, called Puskaravarta-dwipa, is situated Manush yotraparvata, a very lofty mountain which is the extreme limit of the habitable world. No living being has ever gone beyond this mountain. Its base is washed by an immense ocean, in which are to be found an infinite number of islands which are inaccessible to the human race.

The Succession and Division of Time

Time is divided into six periods, which succeed each other without interruption throughout eternity. At the termination of each period there is an entire revolution in nature, and the world is renewed. The first, called Prathama-kala, lasted for four kotis of kotis, or forty million millions of years; the second Dwitiya-kala, thirty million millions; the third, Tritiya-kala, twenty million millions; the fourth, Chaturtha-kala, ten million millions, minus forty-two thousand years. The fifth period called Panchama-kala, the period of inconstancy and change, is the age in which we are now living. It will last twenty-one thousand years. The

present year (1824) of the Christian era is the year 2469 of the Panchama-kala of the Jains.

The comparatively recent date of the commencement of this period seems to me to be worthy of note. I am inclined to think that it is the date of the schism between the Brahmins and the Jains. Such a memorable event may well have been considered as giving birth to a new era. If this conjecture were confirmed it would be easier to fix the time when the principal myths of Hindu theology originated. There is no doubt that the new ideas introduced by the Brahmins into their religion occasioned the schism which exists to this day.

The sixth and last of these periods, the Sashta-kala, will also last twenty-one thousand years. The element of fire will then disappear from off the earth, and mankind will subsist entirely on reptiles, roots, and tasteless herbage, which will only grow sparsely here and there. There will then be no caste distinction or subordination, no public or private property, no form of government, no kings, no laws; men will lead the lives of perfect savages.

This period will terminate with a jala-pralaya, or flood, which will deluge the whole earth, except the mountain of silver, called Vidiparta. This flood will be caused by continuous rain for forty-seven days, which wilt result in a complete upsetting of the elements. A few people living near the silver mountain will take refuge in the caves which are hidden in its

sides, and they will be saved amidst the universal destruction. After the catastrophe the elect will come forth from the mountain and will people the earth. Then the six periods will begin over again, and follow each other as they did before.

The Learning of the Jains

The philosophy of the Jains is contained in four Agamas, twenty-four Puranas, and sixty-four Sastras. The Puranas take the names of the twenty-four Tirthankaras[1], or saints. A Purana is assigned to each of them, and contains his history.

The names of the four are Prathamani-yoga, Charanani-yoga, Karanani-yoga, and Draviani-yoga. These four books were written by Adiswara, the most ancient and most celebrated of all the holy personages recognized by the Jains. He came down from Swarga, took a human form, and lived on earth for a purva-koti, or a hundred million million years. Not only did he compose the Vedas, but it was he who divided men into castes, gave them laws and a form of government, and laid down the lines of social order. In short, Adiswara is to the Jains what Brahma is to the Brahmins; one of them having most probably been modelled from the other.

---

1. Tirthankaras means those who have 'passed over' the gulf which separates human beings from the Godhead.—Ed.

The Sixty-Three Saloka-Purushas

Besides Adiswara, who is the holiest and most perfect of all beings who have appeared on the earth in human form, the Jains recognize sixty-three others, whom they describe by the generic name of Saloka-purushas, and whom they also worship. Their history is contained in the Prathamani-yoga.

These venerable personages are sub-divided into five classes: twenty-four Tirthankaras, twelve Chakravartis, nine Vasu-devatas, nine Bala-vasu-devatas, and nine Baia-ramas.

The twenty-four Tirthankaras are the holiest, and to them most honour is paid. Their position is the most sublime that a mortal can aspire to. They all lived in the most perfect state of Nirvana. They were subject to no infirmity or sickness; they felt no want, no weakness, and were not even subject to death. After having lived for a long time on earth they voluntarily quitted their bodies and went straight to moksha, where they were united with, and incorporated into, the Godhead.

All the Tirthankaras came down from Swarga and took human forms among the Kshatriya caste; but they were subsequently incorporated into that of the Brahmins by the ceremony of the Diksha (initiation). During their lives they were examples of all the virtues

to other men, whom they exhorted by their precepts and their actions to confirm strictly to the rules of conduct laid down by Adiswara, and to give themselves up entirely to meditation and penitence.

Some of them lived for millions of years; the last of them, however, only attained the age of eighty-four.

They were in existence during the period of Chaturtha-kala. Some were married, but the greater number remained celibate, being professed sannyasis.

The twelve Chakravartis, or emperors, recognized by the Jains were contemporaries of the twenty-four Tirthankaras. They shared amongst them the temporal government of Jambudwipa. They came straight from Swarga, and when on earth, belonged to the noble caste of Kshatriyas. Some were initiated into the Brahmin caste by the ceremony of the diksha, completed their lives as Sannyasi Nirvanis, and after death obtained moksha, or supreme happiness. Others returned to Swarga. But three of them, having lived extremely wicked lives on earth, were condemned to the tortures of Naraka.

The twelve Chakravartis were often at war with one another, but they had more especially to fight against the nine Vasu-devatas, the nine Bala-vasu-devatas and the nine Bala-ramas, who all governed different provinces in India.

The second Agama, or Charanani-yoga, contains the civil laws, also regulations relating to social status, caste, etc.

The third Agama, Karanani-yoga, is a dissertation on the nature, order, and component parts of the Jagat-triya.

The fourth, or Draviani-yoga, contains the metaphysical theories of the Jains and several controversial subjects.

Sannyasi Nirvani

The most holy and sublime state to which man can possibly attain is that of Sannyasi Nirvani, which means 'naked penitent'. In embracing this state a man ceases to be a man; he begins to be a part of the Godhead. As soon as he has attained the highest degree of perfection in this state, he frees himself voluntarily, without any trouble or pain, from his own self, and obtains moksha, thus becoming incorporated for ever into the Divine Self. There is no real Nirvani existing in this yuga. Those who aspire to this state must pass through twelve successive degrees of meditation and corporal penance, each one more perfect than the last. These degrees are a kind of novitiate, and each of them has a special appellation. Having at last become a Nirvani the penitent no longer belongs to this world. Terrestrial objects make no impression on his senses. He regards the good and evil,

virtue and vice, to be found on this earth with equal indifference.

He is freed from all passion. He scarcely feels the wants of nature. He is able to patiently endure hunger, thirst, and privations of all kinds. He can live without food of any sort for weeks and months together. When he is obliged to eat he partakes indifferently of the first animal or vegetable substance that comes to hand, however filthy or disgusting it may seem to ordinary people. He has neither fire nor sleeping place. He always lives in the open on the bare ground. Though absolutely naked from head to foot, he is insensible to cold and heat, wind and rain. Neither is he subject to sickness or any bodily infirmities. He feels the most profound contempt for all other men, no matter how exalted their rank may be, and he takes no account of their doings, good or bad. He speaks to no one, looks at no one, and is visited by no one. His feelings, his affections, and his thoughts are immutably fixed on the Godhead, of whom he considers himself as already a part. He remains absorbed in the contemplation of God's perfections, all earthly objects being to him as though they did not exist.

By a long course of penance and meditation the material part of the Nirvani gradually dissolves, like camphor when it is put in the fire. At last all that remains of the penitent is the semblance or shadow of a body, an immaterial phantom, so to say. Having arrived at this pitch of perfection, the Nirvani quits this

lower world and proceeds to unite himself inseparably with the Godhead, where he enjoys eternal and ineffable happiness.

Rules of Conduct

In many respects Jain rules of conduct are similar to those followed by other Hindus, and particularly the Brahmins. The Jains recognize the same observances with regard to defilement and purity. They perform the same ablutions and recite the same prescribed mantrams. Most of their ceremonies relating to marriage, funerals, etc., are the same. In fact, all the rules of social etiquette and the general customs in use in ordinary life form part of their education.

The Jains differ from their compatriots in several particulars, of which the following are the most remarkable:

Under no circumstances do they take any solid food between sunset and sunrise. They always take their meals while the sun is above the horizon.

They have no tithis or anniversaries in honour of the dead. As soon as one of them is dead and his funeral is over, they put him out of their memories and speak of him no more.

They never put ashes on their foreheads, as do most Hindus; they are satisfied with making with sandalwood-paste the little round mark called Bottu, or else a horizontal line. Some devotees put these marks on their forehead, neck, stomach, and both shoulders in the form of a cross, in honour of their five principal Tirthankaras.

The Jains are even stricter than the Brahmins in regard to their food. Not only do they abstain from all animal food, and from vegetables the stalks or roots of which grow in bulbous shape, such as onions, mushrooms, etc., but they also refrain from eating many of the fruits which the Brahmins allow on their tables, such as the *katri-kai,* or brinjal, called *beringela* in Portuguese, the *pudalan-kai,* etc. Their motive is the fear of taking the life of some of the insects which are generally to be found in these vegetables and fruits. The principal, and indeed almost the only, articles of food used by the Jains are rice, milk, things made with milk, and peas of various kinds. They particularly dislike asafoetida, to which Brahmins are so partial[1], and honey is absolutely forbidden.

Whilst they are eating their food some person sits beside them, and, rings a bell, or strikes a gong. The object of this is to prevent the possibility of their hearing the impure conversation of their neighbours, or of the passers-by in the street. Both they and their

1 This resinous gum, the smell of which appears to us so abominable that we have called it *stercus diaboli,* strikes the smell and taste of the Hindus and almost all Asiatics very differently. They consider it to be possessed of an agreeable perfume and an exquisite flavour. The ancient Greeks and Romans shared their partiality for this substance.

food would be defiled if any impure words reached their ears while they were eating.

Their fear of destroying life is carried to such a length that the women, before smearing the floor with cow-dung, are in the habit of sweeping it very gently first, so as to remove, without hurting them, any insects that may be there. If they neglected this precaution they would run the risk of crushing one of these little creatures whilst rubbing the floor, which would be the source of the keenest regret to them.

Another of their customs, and one which, though for a very different motive, might be advantageously introduced into Europe, is to wipe most carefully, anything that is to be used for food, so as to exclude as tenderly as possible any of the tiny living creatures which might be found in or on it.

The mouth of the vessel in which water for household purposes is drawn is always covered with a piece of linen, through which the water filters. This prevents the animal, culae, which float or swim on the surface of the well, from getting into the vessel and being afterwards swallowed. When a Jain traveller wishes to quench his thirst at a tank or stream, he covers his mouth with a cloth, stoops down, and thus drinks by suction. This cleanly custom is highly to be recommended everywhere, apart from the superstition which prompts the Jains to practise it.

The Jains form a perfectly distinct class. Brahmins never attend any of their religious or civil ceremonies, while they, on their part, never attend those of the Brahmins. They have their own temples, and the priestly office is filled by men professing the same tenets as themselves.

Amongst these temples there are some which are richly endowed and very famous. The Jains make pilgrimages to them, sometimes from great distances. There is a very remarkable one in Mysore, at Sravana Belgola, a village near Seringapattam. It is between three mountains, on one of which is an enormous statue, about seventy feet high, sculptured out of one solid piece of rock. It must have been a tremendous piece of work; for to execute it, it was necessary to level the ground from the top of the mountain to below the base of the statue, and there form a sort of terrace, leaving in the centre this mass of rock which was to be carved into the shape of the idol. It is a very fine piece of Hindu sculpture.

Many Europeans who have seen it, have greatly admired the correctness of its proportions. It represents a celebrated Nirvani called Gumata, a son of Adiswara. The figure is absolutely nude, as are most of the idols to which the Jains offer adoration, and which are always likenesses of ancient penitents belonging to this sect. In those days it would have shocked them to represent these penitents as wearing garments, since they

made it a point of duty to go absolutely naked. Childless women may often be seen praying to these indecent idols, in order that they may become mothers.

This temple of Belgola, being only a day's journey from Seringapattam, has been frequently visited by Europeans. It was a great source of grief to the devotees of the sect to see this *punyasthala* (holy place) defiled by a crowd of unbelieving visitors. And what was still worse, these inquisitive foreigners were often accompanied by their dogs and their Pariah servants. In one resting-place they would cook a stew, in another they would roast a piece of beef under the very nose, as it were, of the idol, whose sense of smell, the Jains thought, was infinitely disgusted by the smoke of this abominable style of cooking. At last the guru attached to the temple, shocked at all this desecration, fled from the unhallowed spot, and retired to some solitary place on the Malabar coast. After three years of this voluntary exile, he returned to his former abode on the assurance that Europeans had ceased to visit the place, and that temple had been thoroughly purified.

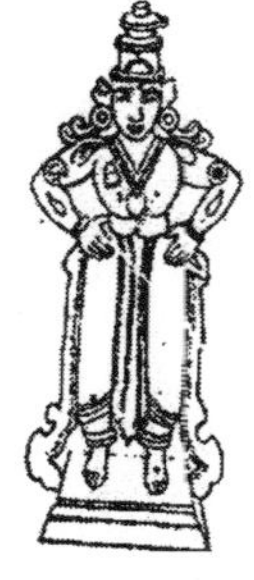

Now, I ask you whether it is not the duty of any well-conducted man, even if he does not respect them, at least not to openly outrage the prejudices, feelings, and customs of any people amongst whom he may happen to be

thrown, no matter how peculiar or ridiculous they may appear to him. What pleasure could be derived, or what good could be gained, by exciting the anger and contempt of those from whom one has nothing to fear, and who cannot retaliate?

An invalid European officer, who was going to the Malabar coast for change of air, on passing near Belgola, was seized with the idea of spending a night in the temple, which he did, in spite of much opposition on the part of the inhabitants. Two days afterwards the officer died on the road, to the great delight of all the natives, who, of course, attributed his death to a miracle, and looked upon it as a direct retribution from their outraged deity. This just and condign punishment, said they would inspire with wholesome fear others who might be tempted to try a similar experiment.

The idols of the Jains differ in many respects from those of the Brahmins. Almost all have curly hair like Negroes. They wear neither ear-rings, necklaces, bracelets, nor bangles on their ankles, whilst the Brahmins, on the other hand, overload the objects of their devotion with such ornaments.

7

Mantras, Sandhya, Sacrifices

The famous mantras, which the Hindus think so much of, are nothing more than prayers or consecrated formulas, but they are considered so powerful that they can, as the Hindus say, unchain the power of the gods themselves. Mantras are used for invocation, for evocation, or as spells. They may be either preservative or destructive, beneficent or maleficent, salutary or harmful. In fact, there is no effect that they are not capable of producing. Through them an evil spirit can be made to take possession of anyone, or can be exorcised. They can inspire with love or hate, they can cause an illness or cure it, induce death or preserve life, or cause destruction to a whole army. There are mantras which are infallible for all these and many other things besides. Fortunately one mantra can counteract the effect of another, the stronger neutralizing the weaker.

The purohits are more familiar with these mantras than any other class of Hindus; but all Brahmins are supposed to be acquainted

at any rate with the principal ones, if this Sanskrit verse, which one often hears repeated, is to be believed:—

Devadhinam jagat sarvam,
Mantradhinam ta devata
Tan mantra brahmanadhinam
Brahmana mama devata.

Which means, 'The universe is under the power of the gods; the gods are under the power of mantras; the mantras are under the power of the Brahmins; therefore the Brahmins are our gods.' The argument is plainly set out, as you may see, and these modest personages have no scruples about arrogating to themselves the sublime title of Brahma, gods, or gods of the earth.

As an instance of the efficacy of mantras, I will cite the following example, which is taken from the well-known Hindu poem Brahmottara Kanda, composed in honour of Siva:

'Dasarha, king of Madura, having married Kalavati, daughter of the king of Benares, was warned by the princess on their wedding-day that he must not take advantage of his rights as her husband, because the mantra of the five letters, which she had learned, had so purged and purified her that any man who ventured upon any familiarities with her would do so at the risk of his life, unless he had been previously cleansed from all defilements through the same medium. Being his wife she could not teach him this mantra because by doing so she would become his guru, and

consequently his superior. The next day the husband and wife both went in quest of the great Rishi, Garga, who, on learning the object of their visit, bade them fast for one day and bathe the following day in the Ganges. Thus prepared the pair returned to the penitent, who made the husband sit down on the ground facing the east, and having seated himself by his side, but facing the west, whispered these two words in his ear, "Namah Sivaya" Scarcely had the king Dasarha heard these marvellous words when a flight of crows was seen issuing from different parts of his body, which flew away and disappeared; these crows being nothing more or less than the sins which the prince had previously committed.'

'This story,' continues the author, 'is really true. I had it from my guru Veda-Vyasa, who learned it himself from the Para-Brahma. The king and his wife, thus purified, lived happily together for a great many years, and only quitted this world to join Para-Brahma, the Supreme Being, in the abode of bliss.'

When one points out to the Brahmins that these much-vaunted mantras do not produce startling effects in the present day, they reply that this must be attributed to the Kali-yuga, that is to say, to the Fourth Age of the world, in which we are now living, a veritable age of iron, when everything has degenerated; a period of calamities and disasters, when virtue has ceased to rule the earth. They maintain,

nevertheless, that it is still not at all uncommon for mantras to work miracles, and this they confirm by citing stories which are quite as authentic and credible as the one I have just related.

The most famous and the most efficacious mantras for taking away sins, whose power is so great that the very gods tremble at it, is that which is called the Gayatri. It is so ancient that the Vedas themselves were born from it. Only a Brahmin has the right to recite it and he must prepare himself beforehand by other prayers and by the most profound meditation. He must always repeat it in a low voice, and take the greatest care that he is not overheard by a Sudra, or even by his own wife, particularly at the time when she is in a state of uncleanness The following are the words of this famous mantra.

Tat savitur varenyam bhargo devasya
Dhimahi dhiyo yo nah prachodayat.

It is a prayer in honour of the Sun, one of whose names is Savita. It is a great mystery. Each word, and indeed each syllable, is full of allusions which only a very few Brahmins understand. I have never met any one who was able to give me an intelligible translation or explanation of them. A Brahmin would be guilty of an unpardonable crime and the most terrible sacrilege if he imparted it to an unbeliever. There are several other mantras which are called Gayatri, but the one mentioned above is that which is most generally used.

After the Gayatri, the most powerful mantra is the mysterious monosyllable Om or Aum. Though it is to the interest of the Brahmins to keep the real meaning of this sacred word a profound secret, and though the greater number of them do not understand it themselves, there does not appear to be much doubt that it is the symbolic name of the Supreme Being, one and indivisible, like the word Aum[1]. This mystic word, which is always pronounced with extreme reverence, suggests an obvious analogy to that ineffable and mysterious Hebrew word Jehovah; guardians of the mantras, many others venture to recite them. In some professions they are absolutely indispensable. Doctors, for instance, even when not Brahmins, would be considered very ignorant, and, no matter however they might be in their profession, would inspire no confidence, if they were unable to recite the special mantra that suited each complaint; for a cure is attributed quite as much to man-tras as to medical treatment. One of the principal reasons why so little confidence is placed in European doctors by the Hindus is that, when

1. The Hindu conception of the word Aum is thus explained by one authority: 'As long as there has been a Hindu Faith the power of sound has been recognized in the Sacred Word. In that word lie all potencies, for the sacred word expresses the one and latent Being, every power of generation, of preservation, and of destruction. . . . Therefore was it never to be sounded save when the mind was pure, when the mind was tranquil, when the life was noble.'—H.B.

administering their remedies, they recite neither mantras nor prayers.

Midwives must also be acquainted with a good many; and they are sometimes called mantradharis, or women who repeat mantras; for there is no moment, according to Hindu superstitions, when mantras are, more needed than at the birth of a child. Both the new-born infant and its mother are peculiarly susceptible to the influence of the evil eye, the inauspicious combination of unlucky planets or unlucky days, and a thousand other unpropitious elements. A good midwife, well primed with efficacious mantras, foresees all these dangers and averts them by reciting the proper words at the proper moment.

But the cleverest mantra-reciters, and at the same time the most feared, are the charlatans who profess to be thoroughly initiated in the occult sciences, such as sorcerers, necromancers, soothsayers, etc. They have in their possession, if they are to be believed, mantras which are capable of working all the wonders which I enumerated at the beginning of this chapter. They recite them for the purpose of discovering stolen property, thieves, hidden treasure, foretelling future events, etc. In a country where superstition, ignorance, and the most extravagant credulity reign supreme, it is no wonder that impostors abound and are able to make a large number of dupes.

The hatred which is felt for these mischievous sorcerers is only equalled by the

fear that they inspire; and that is saying a great deal. Woe to anyone who is accused of having injured another by his spells! The punishment that is usually inflicted consists in pulling out two front teeth from the upper jaw. When bereft of these two teeth, it is thought the sorcerer will no longer be able to pronounce his diabolical mantras distinctly. If he mispronounces the words his familiar spirit will be angry, and the misfortune that he is trying to bring down upon someone else will, it is thought, fall on his own head.

One day a poor man who lived near me, and who had just undergone this painful punishment, came and threw himself at my feet, protesting his innocence and begging for protection and for advice as to how he could obtain justice. The unfortunate fellow certainly did not look like a sorcerer, but as I had neither the power nor the means of interfering in the affair, I could only offer him my sympathy and assure him how indignant I felt at the iniquitous treatment to which he had been subjected.

There are certain mantras which have a very special significance. They are called Bija-aksharas or radical letters; such, for instance, as *hram, hrim, hrom, hroum, hraha,* etc. To those who have the key to the true pronunciation of them and know how to use and apply them, nothing is impossible; there is no limit to the miracles they can perform. The following is an example:

Siva had initiated a little bastard boy into all the mysteries of these radical letters. The

boy was the son of a Brahmin widow, and on account of the stain on his birth had experienced the mortification of being excluded from a wedding feast, to which many persons of his caste had been invited. He revenged himself by simply pronouncing two or three of these radical letters through a crack in the door of the room where the guests were assembled. Immediately, by virtue of these marvellous words, all the dishes that had been prepared for the feast were turned into frogs. This wonderful occurrence naturally caused a great consternation amongst the guests. Everyone was convinced it was due to the little bastard, and fearing worse might happen they all rushed with on accord to invite him to come in. After they had apologized humbly for what had happened he entered the room and merely pronounced the same words backwards, when the frogs suddenly disappeared, and they saw with great pleasure the cakes and other refreshments which had been on the table before.

I will leave it to someone else to find, if he can, anything amongst the numberless obscurations of the human mind that can equal the extravagance of this story, which a Hindu would nevertheless believe implicitly.

Sandhya

Sandhya is performed by pious Hindus once or more times, in a day. Rules to be observed are:

He performs the Samkalpa, then calling to mind the gods of the waters, he worships them. He then thinks of the Ganges, and addresses the following prayer to the sacred river:

'O Ganges! who were born in Brahma's pitcher, whence you descended in streams on to Siva's hair, from Siva's hair to Vishnu's feet, and thence flowed on to the earth to wash out the sins of all men, to purify them and promote their happiness! You are the stay and support of all living creatures here below! I think of you, and it is in my mind to bathe in your sacred water. Deign to blot out my sins and deliver me from all evil.'

This prayer ended, he must think of the seven sacred rivers: the Ganges, the Jumna, the Indus, the Godavari, the Sarasvati, the Nerbada, and the Cauvery. Then plunging into the water, he fixes his thoughts intently on the Ganges, and imagines that he is really bathing in that river.

His ablutions finished, he turns towards the sun, takes water in his hands three times, and makes a libation to the sun by letting the water run off the tips of his fingers.

He then leaves the water, girds up his loins with a pure cloth, and puts another on his shoulders. He sits down with his face to the east, fills his brass vessel with water, which he places in front of him, rubs his forehead with the ashes of cow-dung or sandalwood, and traces on it the red mark called Tilaka according to the custom of his caste. He ends by hanging, either a wreath of flowers round his neck, or else a string of seeds called Rudrakshas.

He thinks of Vishnu, and in honour of him drinks three times a little of the water contained in the vessel. He also makes three libations to the sun by pouring water on the ground.

Similar libations are made in honour of the gods Vishnu, Siva, Brahma, Indra, Agni, Yama, Nairuta, Varuna, Vayu, Kubera, Isana, the air, the earth, and all the gods in general, mentioning those by name which occur to his memory.

Then he rises, pronouncing aloud the name of the sun, and worshipping him. He then meditates some time on Vishnu, and repeats the prescribed form of prayer in his honour.

He again repeats the names of the gods, turning round the while, and ends by making them a profound bow.

Thinking once again of the sun, he addresses the following prayer to him:

'O sun-god! You are Brahma at your rising, Rudra at noon, and Vishnu when setting. You are the jewel of the air, the king of the day, the witness of everything that takes place on earth; you are the eye of the world, the measurer of time; you order the day and night, the weeks, the months, the years, the cycles, the kalpas, the yugas, the seasons, the ayanas, the times of ablution and of prayer. You are lord of the nine planets; you absolve the sins of those who

pray to you and offer you sacrifices. Darkness flies at your approach. In the space of sixty ghatikas (twenty-four minutes) you ride mounted in your chariot over the great mountain of the North, which is ninety million five hundred and ten thousand yojanas in extent. I worship you with all my strength; deign in your mercy to put away all my sins.'

Hereupon he turns round and round, twelve, twenty-four or forty-eight times according as he is able, in honour of the sun.

He then goes to a sacred fig-tree, and with his face towards the east makes it a profound inclination, repeating the following prayer the while: 'O Aswattha tree! You are a god! You are the king of trees! Your roots represent Brahma, your trunk Siva, your branches Vishnu. Thus are you the emblem of the Trimurti. All those who honour you in this world by performing to you the ceremony of the Upanayana or of marriage, by walking round about you, by adoring you and singing your praises, or by other similar acts, will obtain remission of their sins in this world and a home of bliss in the next. Penetrated with the consciousness of these truths I praise and adore you with all my strength. Deign to give me a proof of your goodness by vouchsafing the pardon of my sins in this world, and a place with the blessed after death.'

He then walks round the tree seven, fourteen, twenty-one, twenty-eight, thirty-five, or more times, according as he has strength, always increasing the number by seven.

He then reads some devotional book for a certain time, and having finished he rises, clothes himself with pure cloths, plucks a few flowers to offer to his household gods, fills his copper vase with water, and returns to his house.

Second Part of the Sandhya.

If for any reason the person is unable to perform the ablutions that form part of the first part of the Sandhya, he must at any rate try to accomplish the second part by attentively and devoutly repeating the prayers that belong to it. He first stands with his face to the east or towards the sun. He begins by knotting the little lock of hair which grows on the top of his head, then he takes a little darbha grass in his left hand, and in his right hand a larger quantity which he cuts to the length of his palm.

The Morning Sandhya

He begins his religious exercises with the following prayer:

Apavitraha pavitrova sarva vastram-
gatopiva Yassmaret pundareekaksham,
Sabahiabhiantara suchih.

This means: 'Whether a man be pure or impure, or in whatsoever station in life he may find himself, if he thinks of him who has eyes

like the lotus[1] he shall be pure within and without.'

He then prays to the water in the following words:-

'Water of the sea, of the rivers, of tanks, of wells, and of any other place whatsoever, hear favourably my prayers and vows! As the traveller, fatigued with the heat, finds rest and comfort under a tree's shade, so may I find in you solace and assistance in all my ills, and pardon for all my sins!

'O Water! you are the eye of sacrifice and battle! You have an agreeable flavour; you have the bowels of a mother for us, and all her feelings towards us! I call upon you with the same confidence with which a child at the approach of danger flies to the arms of a loving mother. Cleanse me from my sins, and all other men of their sins. O Water! at the time of the Flood Brahma the omniscient, whose name is spelt with one letter, existed alone, and existed under your form. This Brahma brooding over you and mingling with you did penance, and by the merits of his penance created night. The waters which covered the earth were drawn into one place and formed the sea. Out of the sea were created the day, the years, the sun, the moon, and Brahma with his four countenances, Brahma created anew the firmament, the earth, the air, the smaller

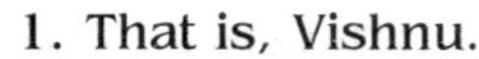
1. That is, Vishnu.

worlds, and everything that was in existence before the Flood.'

This prayer ended, the Brahmin sprinkles a few drops of water on his head from three stalks of the sacred darbha grass.

Whoever in the morning shall address these prayers to water, and shall be duly impressed with their import, will surely receive remission of his sins.

Then clasping his hands, the Brahmin says:

'Vishnu! your eyes are like a flower! I offer you my worship. Pardon my sins; I perform the Sandhya to keep my good name and dignity as a Brahmin.' He then recalls to mind the names of the greater and lesser worlds and the divinities who inhabit them, particularly the fire, the wind, and the sun, also Brihaspati, Indra, and the gods of the earth.

After that he puts his right hand on his head, and recalls to his memory the names of Brahma, of the wind, and of the sun. He then shuts his eyes, and at the same time closing his right nostril with his thumb, he invokes the god Brahma in these words:

'Come, Brahma, come to my navel, and stay, stay there a long time.'

He then fancies to himself that this powerful god is seated on his navel; that the deity is red in colour, having four faces and two arms, a cord round his waist, holding a pitcher in his hand, riding on a goose, and accompanied by

a multitude of divinities. He then thinks of him as having had no beginning, as possessing the key to all knowledge and being able to grant all the desires of mankind, and especially as the head guru of Brahmins, endowed with the fullest power to purify and sanctify them; finally as the Creator of all things, and as an eternal being. After which he says:

'Glory to the earth! Glory to the greater worlds![1]' (These he mentions by name, and thinks of them as all lighted by the sun.) 'May my heart and my will be drawn to the path of virtue; may my desires be fulfilled in this life and in the next. To you, Brahma, who have created water, light, amritam, etc., to you I offer adoration.'

This prayer finished, he breathes heavily through his left nostril, and thereby puts to flight all the sins contained in his body. Then, closing the left nostril with either the thumb or the middle finger of the right hand, he thinks of Vishnu, whom he prays in these terms:

'Come, Vishnu, come to my chest, and stay there, stay there, stay there a long time.'

He then fancies Vishnu seated on his chest. This god is brown in colour, he has four arms, he carries a shell in one hand, the weapon called Sankha in another, in the third a Chakra, and in the fourth a lotus. He rides on the bird

---

1. There are seven greater worlds, the names of which are Bhu, Bhuvar, Svar, Mahar, Janar, Tapah, Satya. The first is the earth, the last the paradise of Brahma. They always add the word loka, which means a place (locus).

of prey Garuda. The Brahmin thinks of him as omnipresent in the fourteen worlds and upholding everything by his power. Then he says:

'Glory to the lesser worlds![1]' (These he mentions by their names.) 'I think of them, of water, and of amritam.'

By virtue of this prayer all his sins are blotted quit.

He then thinks of Siva, whom he invokes as follows:

'Come, Siva, come to my forehead! Stay, stay, stay there a long time.'

He imagines Siva seated on his forehead. This god is white; he carries the Trisula or trident in one hand, and a small drum in the other; on his forehead is a new moon. He has five faces, and each face has three eyes; he rides on an ox. He is represented further as the god self-creating and self-sufficient, as the universal destroyer. Then the Brahmin says:

'Glory to all the lesser worlds!' (These he mentions by name.)

Then he adds, speaking to Siva: 'Destroyer of everything in the fourteen worlds, destroy my sins also.'

Whoever repeats this prayer, and makes the foregoing meditation, will assuredly obtain

---

1- There are seven lesser worlds, the names of which are Atala, Vitala, Sutala, Rasatala, Talatala, Mahatala, Patala. The last is the infernal regions, the lowest of all.

pardon of all his sins and be saved. However, as men are liable to fall into innumerable sins, they can hardly do too much to ensure their being forgiven, and the stain of their wickedness removed. The Brahmin therefore addresses the following prayer to the sun:

'O Sun! who art prayer itself and the god of prayer: forgive me all the sins that I have committed while praying, all those that I have committed during the night by thought, word, and deed; forgive me all those that I have committed against my neighbour by slander or false witness, by violating or seducing another man's wife, by eating forbidden food, by receiving presents from a man of low caste, in a word, all sins of any kind into which I may have fallen by night or by day.'

Whoever addresses this prayer to the sun, and is filled with the conviction of what he is saying and performs the Achamana at the same time, will be absolved from all his sins and will go after his death to the abode of the Sun.

To perform the Achamana he must hold some water in the hollow of his right hand, and put it three times to his mouth. He must touch the under part of his nose with the back of his thumb; then joining his thumb and first finger together, he must touch both his eyes, then joining all the other fingers together to his thumb he must touch his ears, his navel, his chest, his head, and both shoulders. And

before putting the water to his mouth he must always be careful to purify it by repeating over it the following prayer: 'Water! you are of a good taste,' The rest as mentioned before. Passing his hand three times above his head he lets fall a few drops of water on it, and then thrice pours a little on the ground. He draws a long breath, and thus ejects all the sins in his body. He must then recite the prayer which begins with the words: 'O water! at the time of the Flood,' etc., as cited above.

Water should be looked upon as the Supreme Being, and as such adoration is offered to it. Nothing is more efficacious than water to cleanse men from their sins. Therefore one cannot perform one's daily ablutions too often; or at least touch water and think of it, and so obtain a remission of sin. After having thus worshipped, the Brahmin draws a little water into his nostrils, and then shoots it out again. With this water the sinful man also falls to the ground and is crushed under the left heel. Then turning to the east, the Brahmin stands on tip-toe. Raising slightly his hands, the palms turned towards heaven, he makes the following prayer to the sun:

'O Sun! fire is born of you, and from you the gods derive their splendor; you are the eye of the world and the light of it!'

Nothing is more efficacious than this prayer, accompanied by adorations, for turning aside anything that may bring sorrow, or sin, or pain,

and for protection against untoward accident. He must add, still addressing the sun:

'Glory to Brahma, Supreme Being! Glory to the Brahmins! Glory to the Penitents! Glory to the gods! Glory to the Vedas! Glory to Vishnu! Glory to the winds!'

While reciting this prayer he offers the Tarpana, that is, a libation of water, to such of these gods as he names and to all the gods in general. He puts under his feet a stalk of darbha grass, and standing upright, on one foot if possible, he recites the famous Gayatri mantra, which is as follows[1]:

'Come, goddess, come and make me happy: You who are the voice of Brahma, whose name is formed of three letters; who are the mother of the Vedas, who are also the mother of Brahma; I offer you my adoration.' He who thus invokes the goddess Gayatri three times a day will thereby be purified from all his sins.

He then pronounces the monosyllable Aum, and cracks his fingers ten times, while turning round. This is to scare away giants and evil spirits. He must then think again of the goddess Gayatri. In the morning he must picture her to himself as a young girl of extraordinary beauty, resembling Brahma in appearance, riding on

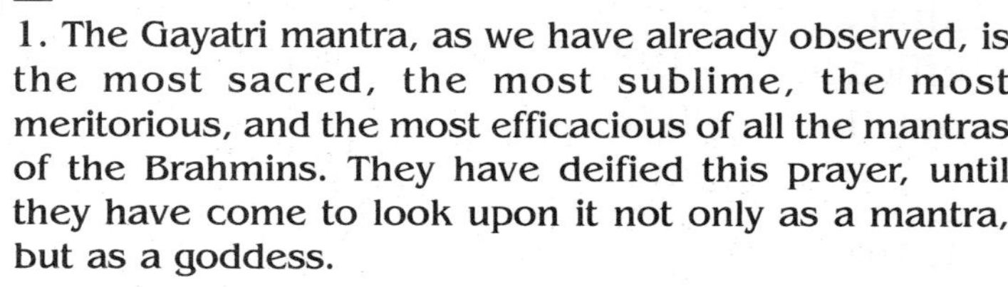

1. The Gayatri mantra, as we have already observed, is the most sacred, the most sublime, the most meritorious, and the most efficacious of all the mantras of the Brahmins. They have deified this prayer, until they have come to look upon it not only as a mantra, but as a goddess.

a goose, holding in her hand a stalk of darbha grass, dwelling in the sun's face and in the ritual of the Yajur Veda. Having thus pictured her in his mind, he prostrates himself before her.

He then addresses Vishnu in these words: 'Vishnu! your eyes are like a flower,' etc., as before.

To recite the Gayatri without having previously offered homage to Vishnu would be labour lost. Such a lapse would indeed be a source of sin. They count on their fingers the number of times that they recite the Gayatri. The hands should be held aloft and covered over with a cloth, so that no one can see how many repetitions have been made. They say it in a low voice so that no one can hear them. The following is the text of this sublime prayer:

'Aum! Glory to Patalal Glory to the Earth! Glory to Swarga! I think of the splendid light of the Sun. May he deign to turn my heart and my soul towords the path of virtue, and to the blessings of this world and of the next![1]'

Every Brahmin ought to recite this mantra from a thousand to ten thousand times daily. He may, if self-indulgent, repeat it only a hundred or even only twenty times, but in no case less than eight times.

It is by virtue of this prayer that Brahmins become like Brahma, and after their death share his happiness. It is so extremely efficacious that its fervent repetition will blot out the most heinous sins, such for instance

1. This is really called Madhya-Vandana.—Ed.

as having killed a Brahmin or a pregnant woman, drunk intoxicating liquors, or betrayed one's most intimate friend, etc. The Brahmin then dismisses the goddess in these terms:

'I have prayed to you, O illustrious goddess, to obtain remission of my sins. Forgive me them, and grant that after my death I may enjoy the delights of Vaikuntha. You have Brahma's face; you are Brahma himself. It is you who have created, who preserve, and who destroy everything. Grant that I may be happy in this world, that joy, wealth, and prosperity may always be my portion, and that after my death my lot may be stilt happier and more lasting! Return, O goddess, after having granted me this favour, return to your usual dwelling-place!'

He offers her Tarpana, or the libation of water, as, also to the sun and to the planet Venus, saying:

'Glory to the sun and to the planet Venus! May the water that I now offer you find favour in your sight!'

He finally addresses this prayer to fire:

'O fire! listen to what I am about to say! Burn my enemies, and those who speak evil of the Vedas! The number of my sins is like a sea of fire, without bottom and without shore, ready to consume me. I implore your mercy, and may it be to me a means of salvation!'

He then evokes Rudra (Siva), whose countenance is like that of time and of fire, and says to him:

'You are the Veda, you are the truth! You are the Supreme Being! Your face is marvellous! You are the face of the world! I offer you adoration.' Then he says:

'Glory to Brahma! Glory to water! Glory to the god Varuna! Glory to Vishnu!'

He offers the Tarpana to each of these gods, and then to the sun, to whom he says:

'Illustrious son of Kasyapa, you resemble a lovely flower! You are the enemy of darkness; through you all our sins are forgiven. I offer you my worship as to the greatest of gods; deign to receive it graciously.' Finally, he turns round three times in honour of the sun, and makes him a profound bow.

The Noonday Sandhya

The person having performed his ablutions and tied up the little lock of hair on the top of his head, traces one of the usual marks on his forehead, and turning towards the east, says:

'Vishnu! the gods delight to look on the beauties of your dwelling-place; the sight charms them, they are never tired of beholding it, they open wide their eyes, the better to be able to contemplate it!'

Then, addressing the sun, he says: 'God of light! God of the day! You are the god of the planets and of all that has life; you are the god who purifies men and blots out all their transgressions, accept the worship that I offer to you!'

He then says:

'Glory to the lesser worlds! Glory to Swarga! Glory to the earth! Glory to Maha-loka! Glory to Tapo-loka! Glory to Yama-loka! Glory to Satya-loka! It is by the almighty power of the sun, the Supreme Being, that water, light, amrita, Brahma with the four faces, and everything that exists, have been created.'

Putting his left thumb on his right hand, he says:

'May everything in me, be it good or bad, commendable or blameworthy, be purified by the sun, the Supreme Being!'

By virtue of this prayer his sins are dried up. Then, closing up both his nostrils, he carries his thoughts back to Krishna, the son of Nanda. This thought causes sin to tremble. He must picture sin to himself under the form of a black man with a horrible face. Then, putting his thumb to his left nostril, he, recalls Siva, and says:—

'Siva, who are the chief of evil spirits, save me from punishment and put my sins to flight with your trident!'

Breathing strongly through his left nostril, he performs the Achamana, and says:

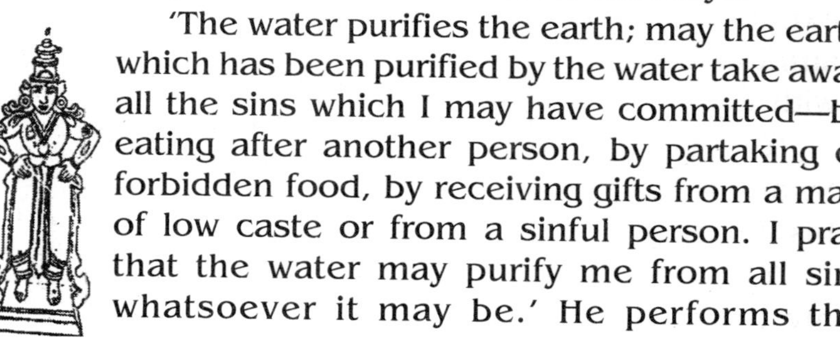

'The water purifies the earth; may the earth which has been purified by the water take away all the sins which I may have committed—by eating after another person, by partaking of forbidden food, by receiving gifts from a man of low caste or from a sinful person. I pray that the water may purify me from all sin, whatsoever it may be.' He performs the

Achamana twice more, for nothing washes away sin more surely then water. Every Brahmin should therefore perform Achamana; for by this act alone not only will all his sins be remitted, even the murder of a Brahmin or of a pregnant woman, but further it also makes him sinless for all time to come. He then takes three stalks of darbha grass, and sprinkles some drops of water on his head with it; but he must first purify the water by reciting over it the Gayatri and the following mantras:

'O water! who are spread on the bosom of the earth, grant that I may perform the Sandhya, so that, being purified by it, I may perform puja!' 'O water! you have a good taste,' etc., and so on as before. He sprinkles some water with the three stalks of darbha grass, first on the earth and then on his head. He who in addition to the above recites the following prayer, may be assured that all his desires will be gratified, that he will live in the midst of plenty and be happy:

'O water! you are in everything that has life, in all quarters of the world, even on the tops of the highest mountains. You are of superlative excellence, you are the light, you are the amrita!' He then rises, and filling both his hands with water, pours it on the ground, saying:

'Glory to Patala! Glory to the Earth! Glory to Swarga!' Then, turning to the sun, and raising his hands on high, he says:

'O Sun! you are the will of the gods, you are the opposite of water! You are the eye of

the gods Mitra, Varuna, and of Fire; you shine in Swarga, on the earth and everywhere!' He then repeats the prayer which begins with these words:

'Glory to Brahma, the Supreme Being!' etc., and so on as before.

He places one or two stalks of darbha grass under his feet, and evokes the Gayatri in these words:

'Come, goddess, come and shower your favours upon me! You are the word of Brahma, the mother of the Vedas; it is from you that Brahma was born. I offer you puja! You are the mother of Brahmins. It is you who bear the engine of the world, and carry the weight thereof. It is through your protection that men live peacefully in the world, for by your care all evil, fear, and danger are kept far from them. It is through you that men become virtuous, and it is from you that puja derives its efficacy. You are eternal! Hasten, great goddess, and answer my prayer!'

It is by virtue of this prayer that the gods have attained to Swarga; that snakes penetrate into the bowels of the earth, and float in the midst of the waters; that fire possesses the power of burning; that Brahmins, grown like the gods, merit daily to receive worship and sacrifice from other men in acknowledgement of their surpassing knowledge and virtue. He repeats the invocation to the sun, and purifies himself in pronouncing the sacred word Aum.

Then he, performs the Vyahriti in the following manner:

'Glory to Patala!'—he puts his hands to his head.

'Glory to the Earth!'—he puts his hands on the tuft of hair on the top of his head.

'Glory to Swarga!'—he touches himself all over his body.

Then he exclaims, 'Aum-bahatu!' at the same time cracking his fingers ten times whilst turning round, and he stamps the ground with his left heel to scare away giants and evil spirits.

He evokes the Gayatri afresh, whom now at noon he represents to himself under the image of Vishnu, in the prime of life, clothed in a golden robe, and dwelling in the sun's face. He then recites the Gayatri mantra the proper number of times, exactly as before described, and then he dismisses the deity, saying:

'You are born of Siva's face; you dwell in the bosom of Vishnu; you are known to Brahma; go, goddess, whither you will! You are Brahma, the Supreme Being; you receive the worship of Vishnu; you are the life of Brahmins; their fate is in your hands; it is in your power to give them happiness in this world and in the next; give me many children, and may I always have abundance of wealth. Illustrious mother! I have offered you puja; now depart whither it seemeth good!'

Nevertheless he says yet another prayer to her:

'Divine wife of Narayana! preserve me from any pain in my head, face, tongue, nose, nostrils, ears, shoulders, thighs, feet, and in any part of my body; preserve me from pain day and night!'

He thus sings the Gayatri's praises:

'You are quick-witted; you are enlightenment itself; you are not subject to human passions; you are eternal; you are almighty; you are purity itself; you are the refuge and salvation of mankind; you are omniscient; you are the mother of all the Vedas, of which you are the emblem; you are also the emblem of prayer. It is to you that all sacrifices must be offered; all earthly blessings are at your disposal; in an instant you can destroy everything. Happiness and misery, joy and sorrow, hope and fear are in your hands; everything is dependent on you. All men pray to you, and at the same time your fascinations cast a spell over them. You fulfil all their desires, and overwhelm them with benefits; to you they owe success in all their undertakings; you put away their sins; you make them happy; you are present in all three worlds; you have three bodies and three faces, and the numeral three is of your very essence!'

He who thus sings the Gayatri's praises will receive his reward; all his sins will be forgiven.

Casting his eyes on liquefied butter, he says: 'O butter, you are the light; by your power everything shines; you are the friend of the gods; you form part of the sacrifices that are offered to them, you are the essence of these sacrifices!'

Then, addressing the Gayatri anew, he says: 'You can be divided into two, three, and four parts; nothing can equal your brilliance; I offer you puja!' He adds:

'O goddess, who dwell on the mountains of the North, you are known to Brahma! Go now whither you will, you are the sacrifice of the sacrifice. It is you who offer it, it is you who receive it. It is you who regulate the offerings, it is you who make them, it is you who receive them; you have yielded the northeast to Siva, and you have taken up your abode in the north-west. If we enjoy light, it is you to whom we owe it, to you who have granted it to us that we may by its aid fulfil our religious duties!'

He addresses the fire in these words:

'O fire! come here; I have need of you for puja; offer it yourself, since you are the emblem of it!'

He says to the water:

'O water! remain on the earth, for the use of us who require you: remain that we may drink you, and come down abundantly to fertilize our land!'

Whoever repeats all these prayers at the midday Sandhya will have all his wishes gratified and obtain pardon for all his sins.

He again addresses the Gayatri as follows: 'I worship you, O goddess, under the image of Brahma. You are the mother of the world; Brahmins offer you puja, and in return enjoy your favours. You have the outward appearance of a stone; but you are indeed the creator, preserver, and destroyer of everything!'

He offers arghya to the sun. To this end he puts water and red flowers, some darbha grass, some sandalwood powder, and some mustard seed into a plated copper vessel. While mixing all these together, he says:

'O sun! you are the most brilliant of all the stars! Vishnu borrows his splepdour from you! You are pure and you purify men; I offer you worship! Glory to the sun! I offer him this Arghya!'

Such, then, is the noonday Sandhya. It is a religious exercise which must never be omitted, but if for any reason one fails to perform it, one must do penance before performing the evening Sandhya. This penance consists in repeating the Gayatri ten times, and offering Arghya to the sun.

A Brahmin who does not perform the Sandhya regularly is not permitted to fulfil any other act of religious worship. It would be quite fruitless for him to offer puja, or Sraddha (the sacrifice for the dead), or to fast or to pray.

The inestimable advantages which the Gayatri mantra procures are proportionate to the number of times it is repeated. Thus for a thousand repetitions you would obtain success in all your undertakings; for ten thousand, the forgiveness of sins and abundance of this world's goods; for twenty thousand, the spirit of wisdom and the gift of knowledge; for a hundred thousand, the supreme grace of becoming a Vishnu after death.

It is considered most meritorious to solemnly undertake to recite the Gayatri for a certain fixed time daily, the credit gained thereby being graduated according to the length of time devoted to the exercise. It depends, that is to say, on the choice that one makes of the three following periods: (1) from sunrise to sunset; (2) from sunrise to noon; and (3) at intervals of about three hours.

Any Brahmin who makes such a vow calls together a certain number of his fellow-Brahmins, and says in their presence:

'Today being such and such a day of such and such a month, I, so-and-so Brahmin, of such and such country and family, being desirous of averting all danger from myself, of growing in virtue, and of obtaining the delights of Swarga after my death, hereby call all present to witness that I vow to recite the Gayatri every day from such an hour till such an hour.'

The Evening Sandhya

Hindus begin this Sandhya about sunset, but it must not be performed on the day of the Sankranti, that is to say, on the day that the sun moves from one sign of the Zodiac to

another, nor on the days of the new, and full moon, nor on the twelfth day of the moon, nor yet on the day on which one has offered to sacrifice for the dead called Sraddha. To perform the evening Sandhya under these circumstances would be committing a crime equal to the murder of a Brahmin. If a Brahmin has just lost his father, his mother or one of his children; if his gums bleed, or if through a wound or accident any part of his body above the navel has been bleeding, or in a word if he finds that he is impure, he would commit an unpardonable sin by performing the evening Sandhya. Indeed, in the last case he would lose all his possessions and his children. Except under these special circumstances, he must never neglect this religious duty, and he must carefully observe the following rules:

He makes the usual ablutions. Then, turning to the north, he recalls the memory of Vishnu. He then thinks of Brahma and addresses the following prayer to him:

'Brahma, you have four faces, you are my creator! Forgive me all the sins that I have committed. I am now beginning the evening Sandhya. Deign to be present, and repose on my chest, and deliver me from my sins.'

He then recites the mantra which begins with these words: 'Glory to the lesser worlds!' and so on as before. Closing up both nostrils, he thinks of Vishnu, and imagines that he is resting on his navel, and says: 'O Vishnu! you are of great stature and black in colour. You have four arms, you are the preserver of all that exists; destroy my sins.' He offers worship to the seven greater worlds, as in the morning Sandhya, and again addressing Vishnu, he says: 'You have created light, amrita, and all that is used for the food of mankind. Preserve me, and preserve all that lives in the world!'

Closing the right nostril with his finger, he breathes strongly through the left, and by this means burns all the sins that are in his body. Then he ejects them by breathing forcibly through the right nostril. He then directs his thoughts to Siva, the destroyer of sin and of all things, and imagines that he is resting on his forehead. He says to him; 'O Siva! you are white and tall. You have the mark of a half-moon on your forehead; you have three eyes; you destroy all things; you are the god of gods; I implore your protection, and offer you worship!' He once more offers puja to the different worlds, and destroys his sins by virtue of the following prayer: 'Oh, may my sins be destroyed by the almighty power of the sun and the fire!' He adds: 'O fire! you are prayer and the god of prayer. Forgive me all the mistakes I have made in the different mantras that I have recited; and forgive me, besides, all the sins that I have this day committed in thought, word, and deed. May this water, which I drink from my uplifted hand, destroy everything bad and sinful that may be in me.' He performs the Achamana, as at the morning Sandhya. He also inhales some purified water into his nostrils, as he did before, and recites

the mantra, which begins with the words: 'O water! at the time of the Flood,' etc., and so on, as before mentioned.

Then he ejects by a forcible expiration the water in his nostrils, which carries away the sinful man[1], whom he crushes at once upon a stone. He represents this man of sin to himself as a powerful being, of extraordinary strength with a red belly, white hair and beard, and a hideous and distorted face.

He evokes the Gayatri, and turning to the west, he says:—

'O god of the day, on whom depends the happiness of mankind, I offer the evening Sandhya: deign to honour me with your presence! O goddess Gayatri, who are the emblem of the Vedas and the word of Brahma, whose name is composed of three letters! I

---

1. Here is another portrait of a man of sin, culled from the Sama-Veda: 'The murder of a Brahmin forms the head of the man of sin; drinking intoxicating liquors, the eyes; theft, particularly of gold, the face; the murder of a guru, the ears; the murder of a woman, the nose; the murder of a cow, the shoulders; the rape of another man's wife, the chest; the wilful production of abortion, the neck; oppression of the innocent and just, the belly; ill treatment of anyone who has sought protection, the stomach; to slander your guru, violate a virgin, betray a secret confided to you, or to be false to anyone who has relied on you, these are the private parts and the thighs; and the hairs of these are the smaller sins. This man of sin is of gigantic stature, and has a horrible face; he is black, and has wild bright eyes; he delights in torturing mankind.'

offer you puja; hasten hither that I may be happy!'

Whilst making this prayer his hands are spread open and raised towards heaven. He then rubs his hands together and puts them to his breast, believing in imagination that the Gayatri is reposing there. He cracks his finger-joints ten times, and turns round at the same moment; and by that he closes all places of egress, so that the goddess cannot depart. He pictures her to himself as an old woman, having Siva's face, riding on an ox, dwelling in the disk of the sun, and united to all the Vedas. Then he says:—

'Divine wife of Siva! you are the mother of all that is. I offer you puja at the approach of night, take me under your protection and save me! Come, Gayatri, come and favourably hear my prayers!'

Whoever recites these words will obtain all that he asks for. Then, facing the north, with his arms hanging down, he recites the Gayatri mantra, in the same manner and the same number of times as before. It is impossible to repeat this prayer too often in the evening, evening prayers being so much more efficacious than others. A Brahmin who daily recites this prayer uninterruptedly from sunset to midnight will by this pious exercise most assuredly place himself beyond the possibility of want or misery, and will ensure for himself a quiet and peaceful death, without sickness or pain, when his long and prosperous career shall draw to a close.

To dismiss the goddess Gayatri he uses the same formulas as those of the noonday Sandhya, and, after the Tarpana or libation of water to the sun and the planet Venus, he addresses Siva in these words: 'O Rudra!. protect me from all accident and danger as well by night as by day. You are the lord of the world; take me under your protection that nothing 'May hurt me or do me harm.' The prayer to fire follows; then he offers Tarpana to the following gods, saying: 'Glory to Brahma! Glory to water! Glory to Varuna! Glory to Vishnul Glory to Rudra!' While offering Arghya to the sun, he says: 'God of light, god of the day! I offer you worship I Receive the Arghya that I now present to you, and deliver me from the cares and dangers of the world.'

8

Priests and Purohits

I shall begin this chapter by giving an accurate description of a true guru or priest belonging to the sect of Siva. This picture is taken from the *Vedanta Sara*, to which it serves as an introduction. At the same time I must warn my readers that it would be difficult to find any points of resemblance between this picture and the gurus of the present day, who are very far from attaining to this pitch of perfection. The sketch will, however, prove that even the very highest moral virtues were not unknown to the Hindus, though now they regard them only as subjects for speculative discussion.

A true guru is a man who is in the habit of practising all the virtues; who with the sword of wisdom has lopped off all the branches and torn out all the roots of sin, and who has dispersed, with the light of reason, the thick shadows in which sin is shrouded; who, though seated on a mountain of sins, yet confronts their attacks with a heart as hard as a diamond;

who behaves with dignity and independence; who has the feelings of a father for all his disciples; who makes no difference in his conduct between his friends and his enemies, but shows equal kindness to both; who looks on gold and precious stones with the same indifference as on pieces of iron or potsherd, and values the one as highly as the other; whose chief care is to enlighten the ignorance in which the rest of mankind is plunged.

He is a man who performs all the acts of worship of which Siva is the object, omitting none; who knows no other god than Siva, and reads no other history than his; who shines like the sun in the midst of the dark clouds of ignorance which surround him; who meditates unceasingly on the merits of the *lingam*, and proclaims everywhere the praises of Siva; who rejects, even in thought, every sinful action, and puts in practice all the virtues that he preaches; who, knowing all the paths which lead to sin, knows also the means of avoiding them; who observes with scrupulous exactitude all the rules of propriety which do honour to Siva.

He should be deeply learned, and know the Vedanta perfectly. He is a man who has made pilgrimages to all the sacred places, and has seen with his own eyes Benares, Kedaram, Conjeeveram, Ramesvaram, Srirangam, Sringeri, Gokarnam, Kalahasti, and other spots which are consecrated to Siva. He must have performed his ablutions in all the sacred rivers,

such as the Ganges, the Jumna, the Sarasvati, the Indus, the Godavari, the Krisna, the Narbuda, the Cauvery, etc., and have drunk of each of these sanctifying waters. He must have bathed in all the sacred springs and tanks, such as the Surya-pushkarani, the Chandra-pushkarani, the Indra-pushkarani, and others, wherever they may be situated. He must have visited all the sacred deserts and woods, such as Naimisha-aranya, Badari-aranya, Dandaka-aranya, Goch-aranya, etc., and have left his footprints in them.

He must be acquainted with all the observances for penance or *asramas*, such as are enjoined by the most famous devotees, and which are known by the names of Narayana-asrama, Vamana-asrama, Gautama-asrama, Vasishta-asrama. He must be one who has practised these religious exercises, and who has derived benefit from them. He must be perfectly acquainted with the four Vedas, the *Tarka-sastra* (logic), the *Bhoota-sastra* (exorcism), the *Mimamsa-sastra* (exegetics), etc. He must be well versed in the knowledge of the *Vedanga* (six auxiliaries of the Vedas), of the *Jyotisha-sastra* (astrology), of *Vaidya-sastra* (medicine), of *Dharma-sastra* (ethics), of *Kavya-nataka* (poetry), etc., and he must know by heart the eighteen Puranas and the sixty-four Kalas[1].

This is the character of a true guru; these are the qualities which he ought to possess, that he may be in a position to show thus the

1. These include all kinds of worldly wisdom.

path of virtue, and help them out of the slough of vice.'

This is what the Hindu gurus ought to be, but are not. What follows is a description of them as they really are. The word guru, properly speaking, means 'master' or 'guide,' and this is why parents are sometimes called the maha-gurus or grand masters of their families, and kings are called 'the gurus of their kingdoms, and masters the gurus of their servants.

The word is also used to designate persons of distinguished rank who are raised to a high position and invested with a character for sanctity, which confers both spiritual and temporal power upon them. The latter, which is exercised over the whole caste, consists in regulating its affairs, in keeping a strict watch to see that all its customs, both those for use in private as well as in public, are accurately observed, in punishing those who disregard them and expelling from caste those who have deserved this indignity, in reinstating the penitent, and several other no less important prerogatives.

Besides this temporal authority, which no one disputes, they also exercise very extensive spiritual power. The Sashtanga or prostration of the members when made before them and followed by their Asirvadam, or blessing, will obtain the remission of all sins. The very sight even of gurus will produce the same effect. Any Prasada or gift from them, though usually

some perfectly valueless object, such as a pinch of the ashes of cow-dung with which they besmear their foreheads, the fruits or flowers that have been offered to idols, the remains of their food, the water with which they have rinsed out their mouths or washed their face or feet, and which is highly prized and very often drunk by those who receive it; in Short, any gift whatever from their sacred hands as the merit of cleansing both soul and body from all impurities.

On the other hand, while the beneficial effects of their blessings or their presents excite so large an amount of respect and admiration from the public, their maledictions, which are no less powerful, are as greatly feared. The Hindus are convinced that their curses never fail to produce effect, whether justly or unjustly incurred. Their books are full of fables which seem to have been invented expressly to exemplify and strengthen this idea. The attendants of the guru, who are interested in making the part which their master plays appear credible, are always recounting stories on this subject, of which they declare they have been eye-witnesses; and in order that the imposture may be the less easily discovered, they always place the scene in some distant country. Sometimes they relate that the person against whom the curse was fulminated died suddenly whilst the guru was still speaking; that another was seized with palsy in all his limbs, and that the affliction will remain until the anathema has been removed; or that the guru's

malediction caused some woman to be prematurely confined; or that a labourer saw all his cattle die suddenly at the moment when the malediction was hurled at his head; or that one man was turned to stone and another became a pig; in fact, they all relate a thousand similar absurdities quite seriously.[1]

If the foolish credulity of the Hindu will carry him to these lengths, can anyone be surprised if his feelings of respect and fear for his guru are equally extravagant? He will take the greatest care to do nothing that might displease him. Hindus have been reduced to such terrible straits as to sell their wives or their children in order to procure the money to pay the imposts or procure the presents that their gurus remorselessly claimed from them, rather than run the risk of exposing themselves to their much-dreaded malediction.[2]

—

1. The ideas oi the Hindus on the subject of the blessings and curses of their gurus are analogous, at any rate in point of extravagance, to those which, according to Holy Scripture, were current in the time of the ancient Patriarchs. Noah's curse on his son Ham and his blessing on the other two, Shem and Japheth, bore fruit (Genesis ix). The value that Esau and Jacob set on their father Issac's blessing is well known (Genesis xxvii); also the bitter regret of Esau when he found that he had been supplanted by Jacob.

—

2. Times are charnged since the days of the Abbe and the gurus in most cases now are the mere hangers-on of rich disciples. They may be able to exercise some influence over ther illiterate and poor, but with the majority of the educated and well to do, their influence is not very great. —HB.

Each caste and each sect has its own particular guru: but the latter are not all invested with equal authority; a sort of hierarchy exists amongst them. Besides the vast numbers of subordinate priests who are to be met with everywhere, each sect has a limited number of high priests who exercise authority over the inferior gurus, deputing to them their powers of spiritual jurisdiction. These high priests have also the right of degrading their inferiors from their position and of putting others in their places. The residences of Hindu high priests are generally known by the name of Simhasana.[1] These Simhasanas are to be found in various provinces of India. Each caste and each sect acknowledges one that specially belongs to it. For instance, the Brahmins who belong to the Smarta sect have a different guru from the Tatvavadi sect, and these again recognize a different one from the Vaishnavite Brahmins.

The different branches of the sects of Vishnu and Siva have also their own particular gurus and high priests. The Sri-Vaishnavas, for instance, acknowledge four Simhasanas and seventy-two Pithas or supplementary establishments, where the junior gurus reside, besides

1. This word may be translated 'throne.' It is derived from the two words, simha, which means lion, and, asana, which means a seat, because a high priest's throne ought to be covered with a lion's skin. Custom, however, has changed this for that of a tiger. —Dubois. Simhasana is more correctly derived from the figure of a lion on the back of the seat. —Ed.

a multitude of subordinate ministers who are also called gurus.

The greater number of the head gurus belonging to the Vaishnavites are Vaishnavite Brahmins, and they appoint the junior clergy of that sect. The most famous Simhasana of the Vaishnavites is in the sacred town of Tirupati. There a kind of arch-pontiff, the Mahant, resides, whose jurisdiction extends over almost the whole of the South.

Brahmins are also, as a rule, the gurus of the various sects of Hindus who are more tolerant than those just mentioned, that is to say, those who worship both Vishnu and Siva.

The high priest or the guru belonging to one sect has no authority over any other. Neither his *prasada*[1], nor his curse, nor his blessing would carry any weight with them; and it is very rarely that you hear of priests overstepping the limits of their own jurisdiction.

People of very high rank, such as kings or princes, have a guru exclusively attached to their households who accompanies them everywhere. They prostrate themselves daily at the guru's feet and receive from him the *prasada,*[1] or gift, and the Asirvada, or blessing. When they travel the guru is always in close attendance; but if they are going to take part in a war or any other dangerous expedition the holy man takes care to remain prudently

1. Prasada means literally serenity, cheerfulness, kindness, favour, etc., and it has come to mean food or anything offered to an 'idol'. —Ed.

behind. He usually contents himself under these circumstances with bestowing his blessing and giving some small present or amulet, which he has consecrated, and which, if carefully preserved, possesses the infallible virtue of averting all misfortunes to which they might be exposed when far from their spiritual guide.

Princes, from motives of ostentation, affect to keep their gurus in great splendour, with the result that the latter's extravagant pomp often exceeds their own. Besides giving them many very valuable presents, they also endow them with land yielding large revenues. Hindu high priests never appear in public except in magnificent state. They like best to show off all their splendour when they are making a tour in their districts. They either ride on a richly caparisoned elephant or in a superb palanquin. Many have an escort of cavalry, and are surrounded by guards both mounted and on foot, armed with pikes and other weapons. Bands of musicians playing all sorts of instruments, precede them, and numberless flags of all colours, on which are painted pictures of their gods, flutter in the midst of the cavalcade. The procession is headed by heralds, some of whom sing verses in the high priest's honour, while the rest go on ahead and warn the passers-by to clear the way and to pay the homage and respect that

are his due[1]. All along the route incense and other perfumes are burnt in the high priest's honour; new cloths are perpetually spread for him to pass over; triumphal arches called tarantulas, made of branches of trees, are erected at short intervals. This magnificent spectacle attracts great crowds of people, who prostrate themselves before the guru, and, after having offered him their respectful homage, join the rest of the crowd and make the air ring with their joyful shouts.

The gurus of rank make a show in proportion to their means. Those who belong to the sect of Vishnu known by the name of Vaishnavas, generally travel on some steed. Some are walking on foot. The Pandarams and Jangamas, priests of Siva, go on horseback or in a palanquin, but their favourite mode of progression is riding on an ox.

—

1. The custom amongst persons of high rank, such as gurus, kings, princes, and governors of provinces, of being preceded on their march by heralds, singing their praises, is very general in India. These heralds give a long account of their master's noble origin, of his exalted rank, of his boundless power, his virtues, and his many excellent qualities; and they admonish the public to pay the respect and homage which are due to so great a personage. This custom, though of Hindu origin, has been adopted by the Mahomedans. It appears as may be seen from the writings of both sacred and secular authors, that the practice of being preceded by heralds dates from very ancient times.—see Genesis xli. 43; Esther vi. 8; and there are several other passages in the Bible where such heralds are spoken of.

Gurus, as a rule, rank first in society. They often receive tokens of respect, or rather of adoration, that are not offered to the gods themselves. And this is not surprising when one remembers that every Hindu is fully persuaded that, under certain circumstances, the gurus have authority even over the celestial powers.

From time to time gurus make tours of inspection in those districts where their followers are most numerous. They sometimes go as much as a hundred miles from their habitual residence. The chief, if not the only, object of the expedition is to collect money. Besides the fines which they impose upon those who have committed some crime, or been guilty of breaking some rule of their caste or sect, they collect the tribute money from their followers which often greatly exceeds their means. They call this method of obtaining money *dakshina*[1] and *padakanikai*[2] (offering at the feet) and no one, is exempt from paying it.

The gurus also increase their revenue by means of taxes, called guru-dakshina, which are levied on the occasion of a birth, at the

1. Dakshina literally means. the sacrificial fee. It has now come to mean gift. The gift to the priest is enforced more or less among the Madhvas; but among the Saivaites and Vaishnavites the priests are more lenient.
2. This word means literally 'offering at the feet.'

ceremony of the diksha (initiation), at a marriage, or at a death.

If these pastoral visits were of very frequent occurrence it is evident that the resources of the poor flock would soon be exhausted. Fortunately, those of the chief gurus, which are the most expensive, take place but seldom. Some make a tour of their districts once in five years, others once in ten only, and others, again, only once in a lifetime.

Some gurus are married, but most are celibates. The latter, however, do not appear to adhere very strictly to their vow of chastity. Their conduct on this head is the more open to misconstruction in that they can have one or two women in their houses as cooks. According to the customs and ideas of the country, for a man to keep a female servant and to have her as his mistress are one and the same thing.

But in spite of this, the common need, who fancy that gurus are not made of the same clay as other mortals and are consequently impeccable, are in no wise shocked at these illicit connections. Sensible people take no notice, but shut their eyes and say that allowances must be made for human weakness.

The Brahmins pretend that they are the gurus for all castes, and that they alone have a right to the rank and honours appertaining to that profession; but, a number of common

Sudras also contrive to raise themselves to that dignified position. The Brahmins, of course, look upon them as intruders, but this does not in the least prevent their enjoying all the honours and advantages which belong to their rank in the caste and sect by which they are acknowledged.

Except when they are making their tours of inspection, most gurus live in seclusion, shut up in isolated hermitages called mutts. They are rarely seen in public. Some of them live in the vicinity of the large pagodas. But the high priests, whose large households and daily hospitalities entail considerable expenditure, generally live in the large agraharas or towns inhabited principally by Brahmins, and for this reason called *punyasthalas*, or abodes of virtue. There they give audience to the numerous members of their flocks who come to perform worship, to receive their Asirvada, (benediction) and their *prasada* (gift), to offer presents, to bring complaints about the infraction of rules and customs, etc. Hindus, on presenting themselves before their guru, first perform, the sashtanga, and then touch the ground with each side of the forehead. The holy man replies to this mark of respect by gravely pronouncing the word 'Asirvada!' On hearing this, his worshippers rise and receive the *prasada* from him, which he gives, whispering the following words, if they belong, to the Siva sect, in their ear: 'It is who am thy guru: and, whom thou art bound to worship.'

The followers of Siva, having thus done homage to their Jangamas and Pandarams proceed to perform a ceremony. They solemnly pour water over the feet of their guru and wash them, reciting mantras the while; then carefully collecting the water so used in a copper vessel, they pour part of it over their head and face, and drink the rest.

The Vaishnavites go through a similar ceremony with their gurus. A piece of food that a guru has already masticated, or the water with which he has rinsed out his mouth, at once becomes scared in their eyes, and is swallowed with avidity.

About ten miles from the fort of Chinnerayapatam a hermitage is to be found, known by the name of Kudlugondur, where a Vaishnavite guru has taken up his abode. This solitary *mutt*, though but a poor place to look at, is visited by a great number of devotees, who go there to offer their homage to the penitent, to receive his Asirvada and prasada, and through them the remission of their sins. I have been informed by some of these pilgrims themselves, that the more enthusiastic amongst them watch for the moment when the old guru is about to expectorate, when they stretch out their hands, struggling as to who shall have the happiness and good luck to catch the superfluous fluid which the holy man ejects.

Gurus sometimes authorize agents to

collect the tributes and offerings of the faithful, and also give them power to impose fines on evil-doers.

After having discharged the duties to their followers which their position imposes, and performed their daily ablutions and sacrifices, both morning and evening, the gurus employ the rest of their time—or they ought to do so if they adhered to their rules—in the study and contemplation of their sacred books. In the case of married gurus the office descends from father to son. Successors to the unmarried gurus are nominated by their superiors, who generally choose one of their own creatures. A high priest is usually assisted by a coadjutor during his lifetime, who succeeds his chief as a matter of course.

To the sects both of Siva and Vishnu priestesses are attached, that is to say, women specially set apart, under the name of wives of the gods, for the service of one or other of these deities. They are quite a distinct class from the dancing-girls of the temples. They are generally the unfortunate victims of the immorality of the Jangamas or Vaishnavas. These priests, by way of keeping up a character for good behaviour, and conciliating the families upon whom they have brought dishonour, put the whole blame on Vishnu or Siva; and the poor gods, as is only fair, are forced to make amends. So the girls are given to the gods as wives, by the aid of few ceremonies; and we know that these worthy gurus enjoy the privilege of representing in

everything the gods whose ministers they are. The women who are thus consecrated to Vishnu are called garuda-basavis (wives of garuda), and have the image of this bird tattooed on their breasts as the distinctive mark of their rank.

The priestesses of Siva are called linga-basavis, or *women of the lingam*, and bear this sign tattooed on their thighs. Though these women are known to be the mistresses of the priests and other dignitaries, still, for all that, they are treated with a certain amount of consideration and respect amongst their own sect.

Purohits

To settle which are lucky or unlucky days on which to begin or put off an undertaking or expedition; to avert, by mantra and suitable prayers, the curses, spells, or other evil influences of the planets and elements; to purify persons who have become unclean; to give names to newly-born children and draw their horoscopes; to bless new houses, wells, and tanks; to purify dwellings and temples which have become polluted, and also to consecrate the latter; to animate idols and install in them their particular deities by the power of their mantras: these are but a few of the duties which come within the province of the Brahmin purohits, whose services are indispensable on such occasions. The most important of their duties, however, is the celebration of weddings and funerals. The

ceremonies on these occasions are so numerous and complicated that an ordinary Brahmin would never be able to get through them all; they can only be learned by special study. Besides, there are mantras and formulas connected with them which are known only to the purohits, and which are described in books of ritual which they take great care to hide from the eyes of all persons outside their own sect. The father makes his son learn these formulas by heart, and thus they descend from generation to generation in the same family.

There are very few Brahmin purohits, and sometimes they have to be fetched from a great distance when their ministrations are needed[1]. If they have reason to expect a generous reward, they will start off at once, or at any rate they will send a son who is welt versed in their ritual. Sometimes ordinary Brahmins pass themselves off as purohits, especially amongst the Sudras, who are not very particular on this point. These interlopers are unacquainted with

1. A purohit is now to be found in almost every village where Brahmins live. He enjoys a *maniam* or free grant of land. In coutse of time the original family is divided into many families of cousins, who hold office and enjoy the *maniam* in turn. The purohit is a Brahmin whose business it is to fix auspicious days for marriages, journeys, and undertakings generally. He presides at the Marriage and funeral ceremonies of Sudras, but not at the marriage ceremonies of Brahmins. The Brahmin who presides at the latter is called *upadhyaya*. A purohit is sometimes called a *panchangi*, or one who has charge of the *panchangam* or almanac, not a very dignified office. —H.B.

the formulas and correct mantras, and so they mumble a few words of Sanskrit or some unintelligible sentences, believing that this is quite good enough for the Sudras. But if the real purohits, who from self-interest are always on the alert, discover that their prerogatives have been invaded and their powers usurped, a violent quarrel ensues between them and their sacrilegious rivals.

One of the most valued privileges of the purohits is the right of publishing the Hindu almanac. The majority of them, being too ignorant to compile it, buy copies every year from those of their brethren who are sufficiently well versed in astronomy to be able to calculate the eclipses and variations of the moon.

This almanac is an absolute necessity to every purohit, since it tells him not only which are the lucky and unlucky constellations, and fortunate or inauspicious days, but also which are the propitious hours in each day; for it is only at these particular moments that the ceremonies can begin at which he is called on to preside. The Brahmins also draw inspiration from this book in predicting happy and unhappy events in life, Numbers of people come to consult them on points like these; and it is not the common people only on whom this superstition has such a strong hold, for princes and persons of the highest rank believe in it even more firmly, if that be possible. There is no one in high position who has not one or

more official purohits living in his palace; and these men act, so to speak, like rulers of the universe. They go every morning and announce to the prince, to his state elephant, and to his idols, each in their turn, all that is written in the almanac relating to that particular day. Should the prince wish to hunt, walk, or receive visits from strangers, and the perspicacity of the purohit discovers in his infallible book that this is an unpropitious moment, the chase, the walk, or the visit is postponed. In large temples a purohit is specially retained to read to the idols every morning the predictions for that day contained in the almanac[1].

The Hindu calendar is known by the name of the *panchangam*, which means the five members, because it contains five leading subjects: to wit, the age of the moon in the

---

1. The *panchangam* Brahmin is one who, by studying the almanac, is able to state propitious or unpropitious times. He gets his livelihood by going certain rounds, day by day, from house to house, declaring the condition of things, as per the almanac, and receiving in return a dole consisting, usually, of grain. He is not held in much respect by his own caste people, but he is much looked up to by other castes. He is consulted by his constituents, from time to time, when they wish to know the propitious period for any undertaking, as starting on a journey, making an important purchase, putting on new clothes or new jewels, or when about to take up a new appointment, or when any other important event is contemplated. He is a Smarta sect; that is, he is really a worshipper of Siva and wears the marks of that god, but at the same time he respects and worships Vishnu.—Padfield.

month; the constellation near which the moon is situated on each particular day; the day of the week; the eclipses; and the positions of the planets. Lucky and unlucky days are also indicated; those, for instance, on which a person may travel towards one of the four cardinal points; for anyone who could safely travel to-day towards the north would probably be overtaken by misfortune if he attempted to journey to the south. There are numberless other predictions of a similar nature in the almanac, which it would be tedious to give in detail.

On the first day of the Hindu year, called Ugadi[1], which falls on the first day of the March moon, the purohit summons all the principal inhabitants of the neighbourhood to his residence, and there solemnly announces, amidst much music, singing, and defacing, who will be king of the gods and who king of the stars for the year, who will be their prime ministers, and who will command the army; who will be the god of the harvest, and what crops will be most plentiful. He foretells, too, whether the season will be wet or dry, and whether locusts or other insects will or will not, attack and devour the young plants; whether the insects and vermin, which disturb the repose of the poor Hindu, will be more or less troublesome, more or less numerous; whether

1. Ugadi is the Telugu New Year's Day. Nowadays there is no music or dancing on the occasion of the purohit reading the almanac. —Ed.

it is to be a healthy or unhealthy year; whether there will be more deaths than births; whether there will be peace or war; from what quarter the country will be invaded; who will be victorious, etc.

Those who ridicule the purohit and his predictions are the very first to have recourse to him if the country is threatened with any great calamity, such as war, famine, drought, etc. Thus powerful is the sway which superstition exercises over the whole land. It is not only the idolatrous Hindus who give credence to these absurdities; Mahomedans, Native Christians, half-castes, and sometimes even Europeans, are not ashamed to consult the astrologer or purohit.

The high-class purohits only expound to Brahmins the oracles contained in the almanac, but many less fortunate Brahmins procure copies for themselves, and reap a rich harvest from the credulity of the lower classes. This method of earning a livelihood, however, causes them to be despised by persons of their own caste, and they only resort to it when other resources have failed. They always quote their favourite axiom: 'In order to fill one's belly one must play many parts.'

The purohits appear to date back to very ancient times. Most Hindu writers mention them, and, if they are to be believed, the highest honours were paid to these Brahmins in times gone by. They and the gurus share

the duty of preserving intact the ancient customs, and it is they who are loudest in condemning those who violate them.

To them also is due the credit of having preserved from destruction all the books of history or of science that have survived the revolutions by which the country has been so often convulsed.

All the purohits are married, and I believe this to be obligatory, in order that they may minister in Brahmins' houses. A widower would not be admitted, as his very presence would be considered sufficient to bring misfortune.

9

The Hindu Sects

I have shown that the ancient Brahmins recognized one Supreme and Almighty Being, possessing all the attributes that reasonable man should ascribe to such a Being. It is impossible to believe that these sages, being thus impressed with the idea of so perfect a Godhead, could have countenanced the polytheism and idolatry. Indeed, it was not long before divided opinions arose regarding the nature of God and the creation of the Universe. Two principal sects were gradually developed, each of which possesses up to the present day numerous adherents among the modern Brahmins.

The first is called the **Dwaita** (twofold) sect, whose adherents recognize the existence of two beings, namely, God and Matter, which He created and which is one with Him. The other sect, called **Adwaita** (not twofold), comprises those who acknowledge but one Being, one Substance, one God. It has a more numerous following than the other, and includes in its ranks the majority of those Brahmins who

profess to be exceptionally learned. Its adepts designate the leading principles of their doctrine by the technical words *abhavena bhavam nasti*, meaning from nothing nothing is made. They maintain that Creation is an impossibility, and at the same time they hold that pre-existing and eternal Matter is absolutely chimerical. From these premises they conclude that all that we call the universe, including all the various phenomena which we see to be comprised within it, has no real existence at all, but is merely the result of illusion, which is known among them as Maya.[1] From the large number of stories which they have invented for the purpose of illustrating this doctrine I have selected the following:

'A certain man, in a dream, imagined that he had been crowned king of a certain country

1. There are, as a matter of fact, three sects. The first is that of Adwaita, or non-dualism. 'The Universe exists, but merely as a form of the one eternal essence. All animate and inanimate things are but parts of the Deity, and have no real existence of their own. Then comes the Dwaita doctrine, or dualism, which holds that 'God is supreme, yet essentially different from the human soul and from the material world, both of which have a real and eternally distinct existence.' A third and important section hold the doctrine of Vaisishtadwita, or doctrine of unity with attributes. This doctrine is like that of Adwaita, holding that the Deity is not void of form or quality; it regards Him as 'being endowed with all good qualities and. a twofold form: the Supreme Spirit, Paramatma or Cause, and the gross one, the effect, the Universe or Matter.—H.B.

with great pomp and circumstance. The next morning, on leaving his house, he met a traveller, who gave him a detailed account of festivities and ceremonies that had actually taken place on the occasion of the coronation of the king of the same country, and of which he was himself an eye-witness. The incidents related by the latter agreed in all particulars with what the former had dreamed. Illusion, Maya, was equally prevalent in both cases; and there was no more reality in what the one man had seen than in what the other man had dreamed. In a word, things that we take for realities are nothing but illusions emanating from the Deity, who is the sole Being with an actual existence. Our senses deceive us in presenting to us objects which do not really exist. These objects indeed are nothing but appearances or modifications of the Deity; that is to say, there is nothing real about them.'

I do not know whether these would-be philosophers deduce from this pernicious doctrine all the consequences which naturally result from it, and look upon God as the immediate author of all the evil as well as all the good that takes place on the earth. Several of them, at any rate, are not ashamed to express this opinion. The Brahmins with whom I have discussed the subject have candidly confessed to me that, in their opinion, neither good nor evil exists; that, in fact, all crimes, even parricide, adultery, fraud, and perjury, are

but acts incited by the divine power; or rather, that these acts are imaginative and are simply the strange result of Maya, a delusion which deceive us and causes us to take the shadow for the reality[1].

The doctrine of Dwaita admits of two actual substances - God, and Matter created by God, with which He is inseparably united. God, according to this doctrine, is impressment. He pervades all Matter and incorporates Himself, so to speak, with it. He is present in every animate and inanimate thing. He does not, however, undergo the least change or the least modification by such coexistence, whatever may be the badness and imperfection of the things with which He is united. In support of this last contention, the adherents of the doctrine of Dwaita cite, for the purpose of comparison, fire and the rays of the sun. They say that fire can be incorporated in every substance, pure and impure, yet it never loses any of its own purity; so also with the rays of the sun, which are never polluted even when penetrating heaps of filth and mud.

According to these sectarians our souls emanate from God and form part of Him; just as light emanates from the sun, which illuminates the whole world with an infinite number of rays; just as numberless drops of water fall from the same cloud; and just as

1. The Abbe's opinion of the Adwaita doctrine is not supported by modern authorities, such as Professor Deussen and Professor Max Muller, who have written of it in the highest terms of praise. —H.B.

various trinkets are formed from the same ingot of gold. Whatever may be the number of these rays, of these drops of water, and of these trinkets, it is always to the same sun, to the same cloud, and to the same ingot of gold that they respectively belong.

However, from the very moment that a soul is united with a body it finds itself imprisoned in the darkness of ignorance and sin, just like a frog caught in the gullet of a snake from which it has no chance of escaping. Although the soul, thus imprisoned, continues to be one with God, it is, nevertheless, to a certain extent disunited and separated from Him. However great and good the soul may be which animates a human form, it becomes from that moment subject to all the sins, to all the errors, and to all the weaknesses which are the natural consequences of this union with a body. The vicissitudes that affect the soul while it is united with a body do not, however, affect that part of its nature which is divine.

In this respect the soul may be compared to the moon, whose image of the moon is reflected to be disturbed, the image also becomes disturbed; but it cannot be said that the moon itself is disturbed. The changes and chances of the soul united with different bodies do not seriously concern God, from whom it emanates; and as to the soul itself, it is immutably, never undergoing the slightest change. Its union with the body lasts till such a times as, by meditation and penance, it attains a degree of wisdom and perfection

which permits it to reunite itself anew, and that inseparably and for ever, with God: that is to say, it ceases to migrate from one body to another.

The soul is said to be endowed with one of the following three gunas, or inherent qualities, sattva, rajas, or tamas—goodness, passion, or ignorance. It frees itself at one time from one, at another time from another, of these inherent qualities, and it attains perfection only after it is entirely free from all of them.

The five senses of the body play the part of councillors and slaves to the soul. For instance, should the soul perceive a desirable object, it is immediately executed. The nostrils are then commanded to smell it, the mouth to open, and the tongue to taste it; and these organs comply with its wishes. Thereupon the object passes into the body with which the soul is united, and the soul is then satisfied. Thus it is the soul that regulates the actions and the movements of the body. It may be compared, in this respect, with a magnet placed on a brass plate beneath which is an iron needle. If the magnet be moved round the plate, the needle follows in the same direction; but if the magnet be removed, the needle at once drops down and remains motionless. The magnet is therefore typical of the soul, and the needle of the body. As long as these two are united, the body is susceptible of motion; but no sooner does the soul quit the body to take up its abode elsewhere than the body becomes insensible, is dissolved, and returns to the five

elements from which it was originally formed. The soul, on the other hand, like the magnet loses nothing of its efficacy, and in whatever body it takes up its abode, always remains the same.

The two great sects of philosophers above mentioned were subsequently divided into six others, known by the general name of Shadata, the **six sects**, or schools. Their names are **(1) Saiva, (2) Sakta, (3) Charvaka, (4) Kapalika, (5) Vaishnava, (6) Buddha.** To strive to purify the soul, to acquire wisdom and perfection, to dissipate the darkness of sin and ignorance, to free oneself from the threading of passion and from the wretchedness of life with a view to union with and absorption in the Great Being, the Universal Soul, the Paramatma or Parabrahma: such are the objects aimed at by these various sects. Each is distinguished from the others by differences of opinion on the nature of perfect happiness and on the means of attaining it.

The different forms of knowledge taught in these schools are known by the following names: **(1) Nyaya[1], (2) Vedanta, (3) Mimamsa, (4) Sankhya, (5) Patanjala, (6) Vaiseshika.**

The first of these schools, the **Nyaya,** founded by Gautama[2], who came from Tirat, near Patna, on the borders of the Ganges, is

---

1. Nyaya is a compound Sanskrit root, meaning literally 'that by which we enter into a thing and draw conclusions.'—Ed.

2. This Gautama is not to be confused with Gautama Buddha, the founder of Buddhism.—Ed.

held to surpass the others in Tarka-sastra, i.e., Logic. It recognizes four sources of knowledge (1) Pratyaksha, or the testimony of the senses rightly exercised; (2) Anumana, or natural and visible signs, as for instance, smoke, which is proof of the presence of fire; (3) Upamana, or the application of a known definition to an unknown object still to be defined; (4) Apta-sabdam, or the authority of infallible texts, which authority they ascribe to the Vedas, so far as religion and the worship of the gods are concerned, and to the maxims of Gautama, their founder, so far as other matters are concerned.

After the study of Logic, the professors of this school lead their disciples to the study of the visible world, and then to a knowledge of its Author, whose existence, although invisible, is demonstrable by the process of Anumana. They gather from the same source proofs of His understanding, and from His understanding they deduce His immateriality.

But although God in His essence is spiritual, they say that He possesses the power of rendering Himself perceptible, and has, in fact, exercised that power. From Nirakara, or possessing no form, He has become Sakara, or possessing form, with a view to shape and animate the world, whose atoms, although eternal, are nevertheless, without His presence, motionless and lifeless.

Man, according to them, is composed of one body and two souls, the one supreme,

called Paramatma, which is nothing else than God Himself; the other animal or vital, known by the name of Jivatma, which is in us the sentient principle of pleasure and pain. Some hold that this is spiritual, others that it is material.

In order to attain supreme wisdom and perfect happiness this sentient principle must be extinguished; its complete extinction leading to union with Paramatma. The various gradations by which this union is attained will be spoken of later on. It begins with contemplation of, and ends in perfect identity with, God Himself. The process of metempsychosis continues in the meantime, the soul never easing its transmigrations from one body to another.

It must here be remarked that by the word Soul the learned mean the Will or else the Ego, the consciousness of Self.

The **Adwaita** school, founded by the celebrated Sankaracharya, is distinguished from the rest by its metaphysics, and, we may add, by the obwscurity of its dogmas. Most of the Brahmins of the present day who wish to pass themselves off as learned men, blindly embrace its principles. True sanyasis are nowadays not to be found except in this school, which is founded on the system of Adwaita.

The characteristic feature of this sect is the belief in the simple unity of the being, who is none other than the Ego, that is to say, the Soul. Nothing exists except the Ego, yet this Ego in its simple and absolute unity is, so to

speak, a trinity by (1) its existence, (2) its infinite wisdom, and (3) its supreme happiness.

But as the capaciousness of Self is not at all in accordance with the sublime notions of this school, they admit another purely negative principle, which, in consequence, has no actual existence. This is the Maya of the Ego, i.e. error or illusion. For instance, I believe I am now writing to you about the Vedanta; but I am mistaken. It is true, indeed, I am Ego, I do actually exist; but you are not You, you do not exist. There is nothing existent in the world, except the Ego. There is nothing Vedanta, nor doctrine, nor any being except the Ego. In imagining to myself that you exist, I am under the illusion of Maya. I am mistaken; that is all: the subject of my illusion does not in fact exist.

Maya, or illusion, makes men believe that they have wives and children, that they possess cattle, jewels, houses, and other temporal goods: but nothing of all this is real. Hindus explain the effects of this illusion very imperfectly by comparing them to a rope coiled on the ground and mistaken for a snake.

True wisdom consists in obtaining deliverance from this illusion by diligent contemplation of Self, by persuading oneself that one is the unique infinite Being, and so forth, without allowing ones attention to be diverted from this truth of Maya.

The key by which the soul may free its illusions of Maya is contained in the following words which these pretentious sages are

without ceasing:—*Aham-Eva-Param-Brahma* that is to say, I am myself the Supreme Being. Thr conception of this idea, they say, should result in actual conviction and lead to supreme blessedness.

The basic principle of the **Sankhya** school, founded by Kapila, is the doctrine of Dwaita; if rejects the Upamana of Logic, and seems generally less pretentious than the other schools. It also teaches that the soul is simply a part of God, and that the wisdom acquired by yoga, or contemplation, ends in either actual or spiritual unity with God.

Kapila recognized a spiritual nature and a material nature, both of them real and eternal. The spiritual nature, by the exercise of the will, unites itself with the material nature outside itself. From this union born an infinite number of forms and a certain number of qualities. Amongst the forms is that of the ego, by reason of which each being can say: I am I, and not another.

As stated above, the qualities are there in number, goodness, passion, ignorance. One or other of these three qualities predominates in all anil l accounts for the differences to be ob them. Another union of spirit, together with qualities, with Matter produces the elements; and a third produces the world as it stands.

Such then, according to this doctrine of the universe, is wisdom acquired, stages of contemplation produces freedom which liberates itself

at one time from one form or quality, at another time from another, by constantly meditating on these three truths:

1. I exist not in anything!
2. Nothing exists in me!
3. I myself exist not!

This is expressed by the combination of these three words:

Nasmeeha-Namama-Naham!

The time comes at last when the spirit has liberated itself from all its forms and qualities. This means the end of the world, when everything, returning to its primitive state, is lost in and identified with God.

Kapila maintains that every religion known to him serves but to draw together more closely the bonds in which the spirit is held, instead of helping it to free itself from them. For, says he, the worship of subordinate deities, who are in reality nothing but the offspring of the most degraded and latest conceived union of spirit with Matter, binds us more closely to the object of it instead of liberating us from it.

The worship also of superior deities, who are in reality only the offspring of the closest union of spirit with Matter, cannot but be in the same way an obstacle to complete spiritual freedom. Such is the contention of Kapila, and one can but conclude that he wished to sap to the very foundations the authority of the Vedas and of the Hindu religion. Indeed, the groundwork of his doctrine seems to bear a very close resemblance to that of Spinoza and other modern philosophers.

His doctrine gives us also to understand that the gods of the Vedas are merely allegorical figures relating to the world itself, as much in its first principles as in its component parts, which are but emanations from or modifications of these first principles.

Kapila rejects in toto the commonly accepted tenets of the Hindu religion, which, according to him, are founded on mythical, wicked, and impious stories. He teaches that everything that tends to cherish the passions, to which one must necessarily yield if they are not surmounted, is calculated to bind the spirit anew to Matter and to prolong its captivity. It is only after having overcome all such passions, and especially those of lust, anger, and avarice, that one can aspire to complete freedom and the supreme blessedness, known as mukti.

The **Mimamsa** school, which recognizes a blind and irresistible predestination, professes absolute toleration with regard to other sects. Its adepts scrutinize and discuss the dogmas of these sects, without condemning them or venturing on any decided opinion with regard to them. They commend the utmost tolerance in matters of opinion, and affirm that every sect—nay, every religion—pursues the same end, happiness, although they may differ as to the means of attaining it.

There are a number of orgies in the **Sakti-puja**, practised by the votaries of the Sakta

sect. The Saivas are all worshippers of Siva and Bhavani conjointly, and they adore the linga or compound type of this god and goddess, as the Vaishnavas do the image of Lakshmi-narayana. There are no exclusive worshippers of Siva besides the sect of naked Gymnosophists called Lingis; and the exclusive adorers of the goddess are the Saktas.

In this last-mentioned sect, as in most others, there is a right-handed and decent path, and a left-handed and indecent mode of worship; but the indecent worship of this sect is most grossly so, and consists of unbridled debauchery with wine and women. This profligate sect is supposed to be numerous, though unavowed. In most parts of India, if not in all, they are held in deserved detestation; and even the decent Saktas do not make public profession of their tenets, nor wear on their foreheads the mark of the sect, lest they should be suspected of belonging to the other branch of it. The sacrifice of cattle before idols is peculiar to this sect.

There is another sect called **Buddha**, which has no Brahmin adherents at all, its followers being chiefly Buddhists, whose number at present is very small in India. Their doctrine is pure materialism. Spinoza and his disciples endeavoured to palm it off as a new invention of their own; but the atheists of India recognized this doctrine many centuries before them, and drew from it pretty much the same deductions which their European brethren afterwards drew, and which have been

propagated in modern times with such deplorable success.

According to this doctrine, there is no other god but Matter, which is divided into an infinite number of substances, forming as many deities according to some, and forming but one god according to others. They hold that there can be neither vice nor virtue during life; neither heaven nor hell after death. The truly wise man, according to them, is he who enjoys every kind of sensual pleasure, who believes in nothing that is not capable of being felt, and who looks upon everything else as chimerical.

There are also other sects, not so well known; and among them is the **Nastika** sect, whose fundamental doctrine consists in absolute pyrrhonism or scepticism; and also the **Lokayata** sect, whose adherents recognize no difference of condition amongst mankind, no precepts relating to pollution and purification, and who are, moreover, accused of devoting themselves to witchcraft and enchantments.

I will now speak about the **two great sects of the Sudras**. It will be seen that they are far from being as calm and tolerant over points of doctrine as the Brahmins. As a general rule, Hindus profess to pay equal honour to the two great divinities of the country, Vishnu and Siva, without showing preference for either, though there are a great many sectarians who devote themselves exclusively to the worship of one or the other.

The one sect is usually called **Vishnu-bhaktas**, which means votaries of Vishnu; the other is called **Siva-bhaktas**, or Votaries of Siva. The latter sect is also called Lingadharis or **Lingayats** and the former **Namadharis**. These names are derived from the distinguishing marks which the sectarians wear. The followers of Vishnu wear the emblem called Namam, which they paint on their foreheads. It consists of three lines, one perpendicular and two oblique, meeting at the base, and thus forming a sign which resembles a trident. The centre line is red, the two outer lines are white and are painted on with a sort of clay called Namam; hence the name given to this emblem. The distinctive sign of the Saivaites is, generally speaking, the lingam. They sometimes wear it fastened to the hair or round the arm, enclosed in a little-silver tube; but more often they hang it round the neck, and the silver box containing it rests on the chest.

Instead of the Namam, some devotees of Vishnu paint a single red perpendicular line in the middle of their foreheads in a distinctive manner; and instead of the lingam many of the votaries of Siva rub their foreheads and

1. It is impossible to conceive anything more obscene than the meaning of these two marks of Hindu worship, namely, the lingam and the namam; obscene, that is, from the European point of view. From the Hindu point of view they symbolise spiritual and religious truths connected with the divine origin and generation of mankind.—Ed.

various parts of their bodies with the ashes of cow-dung by way of showing their devotion.

The special devotees of Vishnu are to be found if great numbers in the southern provinces of India, where they are known by various names, such as Dasari, Ramanjogi, Bairagi, and many others.

Besides the Namam, which is an unmistakable sign of this sect, most of the devotees may also be distinguished by the extraordinary costume that they affect. The clothes which they wear are dyed a deep yellow, shading into red; many cover their shoulders with a coloured work blanket, which they partly use as a cloak; their turbans, too, are composed of a motley of many hues. Some wear a cheetah's skin on their shoulders instead of the blanket. Most of them have long necklaces of black seeds, the size of nuts. Besides this costume, the devotees of Vishnu always carry a bronze gong and a conch shell called a Sankh; when they are travelling or begging. Both of these are used to make a noise and to announce their approach. With one hand they strike the gong with a little drumstick, producing a bell-like sound; with the other they hold the Sankh to their mouth, and blow through it shrill and piercing sounds, which are very monotonous. These two objects are always to be seen in the hands of those followers of Vishnu who are beggars by profession, and who in some way resemble the mendicant friars of old. On their breasts they wear a sort of brass plate, on which is engraved

a likeness of the monkey Hanumana, or else one of the Avatars, or incarnations of Vishnu. Some of them wear a number of little bells either hanging from their shoulders or on their legs, the tinkling of which warns people of their approach. To all the above paraphernalia some add an iron rod, at each end of which hangs a little brazier of the same metal containing the fire for burning the incense of which their sacrifices are composed.

To ask for alms is looked upon as a right, and even an inherent duty in this sect; indeed as a rule in India anyone who assumes the cloak of religion can practise begging as a profession.

It is principally when they are making pilgrimages to some sacred spot that these religious beggars make use of their privileges. Sometimes you meet as many as a thousand in one party. They scatter themselves through the various villages within reach of their route, and each inhabitant takes in a certain number of them, so that all travelling expenses are saved. This is the only occasion on which they travel in such large numbers, though they never wander about quite alone. Their manner when demanding alms is most insolent and audacious, and often threatening. If their demands are not instantly complied with, they will noisily repeat their request, striking their gongs and producing the most deafening sounds from their Sankhs all the time. If such methods are not successful, they have been known to force their way into a house, and

damage everything they can find. These religious mendicants generally pursue their begging to an accompaniment of singing and dancing. Their songs are a species of hymns in honour of their deities; and they very often sing different ballads. The more freely the latter are interlarded with obscenities, the better are they calculated to attract offerings from the public.

The intemperance to which these religious beggars, and indeed all the devotees of Vishnu, are addicted, causes the better class of Hindus to regard them with great disfavor. In fact such mendicants seem rather to pride themselves on their want of moderation in eating and drinking; from a feeling of opposition to the Lingayats, and in order to make the difference between themselves and their adversaries more apparent. The sobriety of the latter equals, if it does not surpass, that of the Brahmins. Vaishnavites eat all kinds of meat ostentatiously, and drink arrack, toddy, or any other intoxicating liquors or drugs that they can procure. Excesses of all kinds are laid to their charge, and it is amongst them that most abominable rite called Sakti-puja is practised.

The chief objects of veneration amongst the votaries of Vishnu are the monkey, the bird of prey called Garuda, and the cobra. Should anyone be so imprudent as to kill, or even injure, anyone of these creatures in their presence, he might find the consequences very unpleasant, and he would only be able to expiate this supposed crime by offering the

sacrifice called Pavada, which is only performed on very grave occasions, or when it is a question of obtaining reparation for an injury done to some member of the sect, but felt to reflect on all the others. This expiatory sacrifice is a serious affair; for it consists in immolating a human victim, and then resuscitating him.

When it is reported that any person has committed such an offence as renders the Pavadam necessary, all the Vishnu-bhaktas flock in crowds to the culprit's house, round which as many as 2,000 and more have been known to assemble, each of them provided with his gong and his Sankh. They begin by arresting the person who is the cause of the assemblage; and then they erect at a short distance from the house a small tent, which is quickly surrounded by many rows of Vaishnavites. The chiefs select some member of the sect who is willing to be sacrificed, and he is exhibited to the crowd who have come to witness the spectacle.

They make a slight incision in his arm from which blood flows, and the victim then appears to grow weaker and weaker, until he falls fainting to the ground, where he remains motionless. The victim, who of course is only feigning death, is then carried to the tent which has been erected for the purpose, and around which the Vishnu-bhaktas group themselves, taking great care that no one shall approach who does not belong to their sect. Others watch the cause of him who has been the

cause of the ceremony. All this time the whole multitude are shouting and screaming at the top of their voices, which, added to the banging of the gongs and the harsh and lugubrious notes of the Sankhs, produces a din and confusion of sounds as indescribable as they are unbearable. This fearful hubbub continues until the offending party has paid the fine imposed on him, which is generally far beyond his means.

However, the inhabitants of the village and neighbourhood, exasperated beyond all measure, usually try and make same agreement with the leader of the fanatics and, paying them part of the stipulated sum, entreat them to bring the ceremony of the Pavadam to a speedy termination, and to return to their homes. When their demands have been satisfied the headmen retire to the tent, and restore the dead man to life. To bring about this miracle an incision is made in the thigh of somebody amogest them. The blade which flaws from it is collected in a vessel, and then sprinkled over the body of the victim. By virtue of this simple ceremony the pretended dead man comes back to life, in the best possible health. He is then again shown to the spectators, who appear thoroughly convinced of the reality of this marvellous resurrection.

In order to consummate the expiation of the crime or offence which has given rise to the ceremony, they give a great feast with the money derived from the fine, and every one departs as soon as it is over.

I once saw the Pavadam celebrated with much solemnity in a village near my house. The offence which provoked it arose from an inhabitant of the village having unintentionally felled a tree called *kaka-mara* which bears yellow flowers, and to which the followers of Vishnu offer sacrifices and worship.

The **sect of Siva** is just as numerous as that of Vishnu. It predominates altogether in several South. In the western parts of the South, along the whole length of the long chain of mountains which separates what are known as Malabar and Coromandel, the followers of Siva form at least half of the population for a distance extending for more than 100 miles from north to south.

Like the Brahmins they abstain from all animal food and from everything that has had even a germ of life, such as eggs, etc., some vegetable products being included under this head. Instead of burning their dead, as do most Hindus, they bury them. They do not recognize the laws relating to defilement which are generally accepted by other castes, such, for instance, as those occasioned by a woman's periodical ailments, and by the death and funeral of relations. They have also other rules and regulations which differ from those generally in force. Their indifference to all such prescriptive customs relating to defilement and cleanlines has given rise to a Hindu proverb which says: 'There is no river for a Lingayat;

meaning that the members of this sect do not recognize, at all events on many occasions, the virtues and merits of ablutions.'

The point in the creed of the Saivaites which appears to me to be most remarkable is their entire rejection of that fundamental principle of the Hindu religion, Punarjanma, or metempsychosis. In consequence of their peculiar views on this point they have no anniversary festivals, to commemorate the dead and to afford them the benefit of the prayers, sacrifices, and intercessions of the living. A Lingayat is no sooner buried than he is forgotten.

Amongst the Saivaites there also exists a sect known by the name of **Virasaiva**, which refuses to recognize any caste distinctions, maintaining that the lingam makes all men equal. If even a Pariah joins the sect he is considered in no way inferior to a Brahmin. Wherever the lingam is found, there, they say, is the throne of the deity, without distinction of class or rank. The Pariah's humble hut containing this sacred emblem is far above the most magnificent palace where it is not.

The direct opposition of their religious tenets and rules of life to those of all other Hindus, and especially to those of Brahmins, renders the Lingayats peculiarly obnoxious in the eyes of the latter, who cannot endure the sight of the Jangamas and other headmen of the sect. Amongst the Lingayats, as amongst the Namadharis, are an Immense number of

religious beggars, Pandarams, Voderus, Jangamas, etc. Many of these penitent Saivaites have no other means of subsistence except begging. They ply their trade systematically and in gangs. Some, however, live, in retreat in the mutts (monasteries) or temples, which usually possess lands, the rents of which, added to the offerings of the faithful, are sufficient to maintain them.

The gurus, or priests of Siva, who are known in the western provinces by the name of Jangamas, are for the most part celibates. They have a custom which is peculiar to themselves, and curious enough to be worth remarking. When a guru travels about his district, he lodges with some member of the sect, and the members contend amongst themselves for the honour of receiving him. When he has selected the house he wishes to stay in, the master and all the other male inmates are obliged, out of respect for him, to leave it, and go and stay elsewhere. The holy man remains there day and night with only the women of the house, whom he keeps to wait on him and cook for him, without creating any scandal or exciting the jealousy of the husbands. All the same, some scandal-mongers have remarked that the Jangamas always take care to choose a house where the women are young.

The costume worn by the ascetics of Siva is very much the same as that of the Vaishnavites. Both are equally peculiar in their attire. They always wear clothes of *kavi* colour, that is to say, dark yellow verging on red. This colour is obligatory, not only on the devotees of both Vishnu and Siva, but also on everyone who is under a vow of penance. It is the colour affected by all gurus and Hindu priests of all denomina-tions, by fakirs, also by all the priests and religious followers of Buddha who live on the other side of the Ganges.

Besides the lingam, there are several other outward signs by which the devotees of Siva may be recognized, such as the long necklaces of seeds called *rudrakshas,* which resemble a nutmeg in size, colour and nearly in shape; also the cow-dung ashes with which they besmear their forehead, arms, and various other portions of the body. The two chief objects of their devotion are the lingam and the bull.

Though children usually follow the religion of their fathers, they do not become Vaishnavites or Lingayats merely by right of birth. They are only admitted to the sect that their parents belong to when they have reached a certain age, and after being initiated, by the guru. This ceremony of initiation is called diksha. It consists in repeating certain appropriate mantras, or prayers, over the neophyte, and whispering some secret instructions in his ear. But these are all spoken in a language which is seldom understood even by the person who presides at the ceremony.

By the diksha the new member acquires a perpetual right to all the privileges of the sect into which he has been admitted. Persons of all castes can become Vaishnavites and after their admission can wear the Namam or distinctive mark and their foreheads. Neither Pariahs nor even Checkers are excluded; and it has been noticed that the lower castes are particularly numerous in this sect.

I do not think there would be any greater difficulty in becoming a member of the Siva sect, but as on initiation the members undertake to entirely give up eating meat and drinking any intoxicating liquor, the lower castes, who do both unhesitating, find the conditions too hard. Consequently, only high-class Sudras and scarcely any Pariahs belong to this sect. It is no uncommon thing for people to change from one sect to the other, according as it suits their interest, or even out of spite or caprice. Either sect will take a convert from the other without asking any questions or making any difficulty. Sometimes one comes across missionaries scouring the country with written professions of faith in their hands, and using various means for gaining proselytes to their respective sects.

In some parts a remarkable peculiarity is to be observed in reference to these two sects. Sometimes the husband is a Vaishnavite and bears the Namam on his forehead, while the wife is a follower of Siva and wears the lingam.

The former eats meat, but the latter may not touch it. This divergence of religious opinion, however, in no way destroys the peace of the household. Each observes the practices of his or her own particular creed, and worships his or her god in the way that seems best, without any interference from the other. At the same time, each sect tries its best to magnify its own particular deity and to belittle that of its rivals. The devotees of Vishnu declare that the preservation of the universe is entirely due to him, and that to him Siva owes both his birth and existence, since Vishnu saved him several times under such circumstances that without his aid Siva must infallibly have perished. Therefore Vishnu is immeasurably above Siva in every respect, and to him alone should homage be offered.

The devotees of Siva, on their side, maintain obstinately that Vishnu is of no account, and has never committed any but the basest actions, which, only disgrace him and make him hateful in the eyes of men. As proofs of their assertions they point to several facts in the life of this deity, which their adversaries cannot deny, and which certainly do not redound to his credit. Siva according to them, is sovereign lord of all, and therefore the proper object of all worship.

According to the Vaishnavites, it is the height of all abomination to wear the lingam. According to their antagonists, whoever is

decorated with the Namam will be tormented in hell by a sort of fork similar in form to this emblem. These mutual recriminations often end in violent altercations and riots. The numerous bands of religious mendicants of both sects are specially apt to provoke strife: one may sometimes see these fanatics collected together in crowds to support their opinion of the super-excellence of their respective doctrines, They will overwhelm each other with torrents of abuse and obscene insults, and pour forth blasphemies and imprecations, on one side against Siva, on the other against Vishnu; and finally they will come to blows. Fortunately, blood is seldom shed on these battle-fields. They content themselves with dealing each other with their fists, knocking off each other's turbans, and much tearing of garments. Having thus given vent to their feelings, the combatants separate by mutual consent.

That these religious dissensions do not set the whole country ablaze, or occasion those crimes of all kinds which were for centuries the result of religious fanaticism in Europe and elsewhere, is due no doubt to the naturally mild character of the Hindus, and especially to the fact that the greater number compound with their consciences and pay equal honour to Vishnu and Siva. Being thus free from any bias towards either party, the latter serve as

arbitrators in these religious combats, and often check incipient quarrels.

There is no doubt, however, that these controversies were wont to excite general ferment in several provinces at no very remote date. The agitation, excited In the first instance by fanatical devotees, was further fomented by the Rajas and other princes, who became to Vaishnavites or Saivaites according as it suited their political interests.

Those who are acquainted with the character and position of the Bairagis and Gosais of the north, and of the Dasari, Jangamas, and Pandarams in south, are fully persuaded that it would still be quite easy for two ambitious and hostile princes to arm these fanatics and persuade them to come to blows if they raised the standard of Basava (the bull) on one side and of Hanumanta (the monkey) on the other.

In these religious squabbles, which still take place occasionally, the Vaishnavites appear to be the more fanatical and fervent, and they are almost always the aggressors. The reason is, that this sect draws most of its members from the very dregs of society, and so takes a delight in creating troubles or disturbances. The followers of Siva, on the other hand, who belong to the upper classes of the Sudras, are much more peaceable and tolerant.

Hindu Religion and Mythology

The majority of the Hindus, and particularly the Brahmins, take no part whatever in these religious squabbles, The latter act on the principle of paying equal honour to the two chief deities of the country, and though, as a rule, they appear to have a preference for Vishnu, they never let a day pass without offering in their own houses a sacrifice to the lingam, which is Siva's emblem.

It is very difficult to determine the origin of these two sects. Some authors have thought that they are quite a modern institution. Yet they are alluded to in several of the most ancient Puranas. One of the Avatars, or incarnations, of Vishnu, called Narasimha, that is to say, half-man half-lion, is the form under which this deity disguised himself when he came to deliver the earth from the giant Hiranyakashpya, who was ravaging it. We learn in the Bhagavata that this cruel monster had a good son called Prahlada, who belonged to the Vaishnavite sect, and who made the greatest efforts to induce his father to embrace his special form of religion, but without success. However, the ill-feeling between the two sects seems not to have been so marked at the beginning.

Brahmins in general look upon the Vaishnavite Brahmins who profess a special devotion for Vishnu if they do not worship him exclusively, as detestable schismatics. The preference that the latter show for a sect

composed almost entirely of Sudras and the lowest of the people, and thief practice of appearing in public with their foreheads decorated with the Namam, just like common Pariahs or Chucklers, are all offences which degrade them in the eyes of their noble conferers.

No doubt the same contempt would be felt of Brahmins who wore the lingam, but I have never seen one thus decorated, and I doubt whether one could be found anywhere in the south, from the banks of the Kistna to Kanya Kumari. I have been told, however, that there are some districts in the north where persons of this caste are to be found who devote themselves exclusively to the worship of Siva, and who always wear the emblem of this deity.

The sect of Vaishnavite Brahmins appears to have originated in Dravida or Aravam the Tamil country. From there they spread over the provinces up to the Kistna, where they have retained, to the present day, their own peculiar customs and language, as well as their own cult. The Brahmins who inhabit the country north of this river have never permitted these stubborn schismatics to settle amongst them.

The feeling of aversion which orthodox Brahmins entertain for the Vaishnavite Brahmins is shared by Hindus of all castes. A stigma of reproach appears to cling to them. It cannot be the case, however, that the disfavour

with which they are regarded is entirely due to their exclusive worship of Vishnu. I think it must be largely imputed to their excessive pride and arrogance, their extreme severity, and their supercilious manners; for though all Brahmins share these characteristics, it is generally acknowledged that the Vaishnavites display them in an intensified form.

Be the reason what it may, there is no denying that the Vaishnavites form a class by themselves in society. The antipathy which these two orders of Brahmins feel for each other is noticeable on all occasions. The members of one sect never invite members of the other to eat with them, or to participate in their civil or religious feasts; and when one of them is raised to a position of authority, it is on persons of his own sect that his patronage is bestowed.

The two sects of Vaishnavites and Saivaites are each subdivided into several others, which are known under the general term of Mattas or Mattancharas. Amongst the Vaishnative, for instance, there are the Vaishnavas, the Tatvadis, the Ramojus, the Satanis, etc. sub-sects which again are divided into a great many others. For instance, amongst the Vaishnavas there are the Vaishnava-trimalas, the Chandalas, the Nallaris, etc.

The Jogis, the Jangamas, the Voderus, the Viraktas, the Bolu-Jangamas, the Virasaivas etc. belong to the Saivaites.

Each of these sub-sects has Its own peculiar tenets, mysteries, mantras, sacrifices; in fact, some points of variation in rites as in doctrines. The heads of these sub-sects dislike and avoid each other. They often quarrel over the various points of doctrine which cause such divisions. But these are forgotten, or, at any rate, allowed to remain in abeyance, should it be necessary to make common cause in defending the interests of the sect as a whole, during the disputes which occasionally arise between the Vaishnavites and Saivaites.

10

Hindu Temples

Buildings dedicated to religious worship are extremely numerous in India. There are few villages or hamlets which have not at least one. It is even a generally perceived opinion that no place should be inhabited where there is no temple, for otherwise the inhabitants would run grave risks of misfortune.

Among the good works expected of the rich, one of the most honourable and most meritorious consists in spending a part of their fortune in the construction and endowment of these sacred buildings. Such munificence, it is argued, is an infallible means of obtaining the protection of the gods, remission of one's sins and admission into an Abode of Bliss after death. But vanity, ostentation, and desire to attract attention are much more powerful factors, if indeed they are not the only ones that excite beneficence on the part of the wealthy.

Besides the temples with which all villages are provided, one finds many erected in isolated spots, in woods, on the highways, in the middle of rivers, on the borders of tanks

and other large reservoirs, and especially on the summits of steep rocks, mountains, and hills. This practice of constructing buildings onsecrated to religious worship upon elevated sites must have struck all persons who have travelled in India. In fact there are few mountains where a well or a spring is to be found, that are not surmounted by a building of this sort. The choice of sites like these does not appear to be a matter of caprice. We know that the same practice exists among the majority of Asiatic nations. Not only the ancient heathen peoples, but even the children of Israels always chose elevated sites for purposes of religious worship. When God ordered the Israelites to take possession of the land of Canaan, He commanded them above all things to destroy the heathen temples erected on mountains and other lofty spots, to break in pieces the idols, and to destroy the sacred groves with which those buildings were surrounded, as are those of the Hindus to this day. Holy Scripture refers often to these high places and sacred groves.

One can only offer conjectures regarding this custom of placing on elevated sites the temples dedicated to the sacrifices and vows which the people addressed to their gods. Some authors have remarked that the worship of the stars having always been more or less a part of pagan ritual, the heathen constructed their temples so as to face the east at a certain elevation, in order that the rising sun might flood the interior of the temples with its light

and cast its rays upon the religious ceremonies which take place at that time of day[1]. No doubt, too, they thought they were thereby approaching as near as possible to the heavenly powers whom they invoked. Furthermore, the duties of the soothsayers often necessitated such elevated positions, in order that they might see the heavens clearly.

Besides the temples of idols which one meets with at every step in India, statues of stone, of baked earth, and especially of granite, representing objects of popular worship, may be seen on the high-roads, at the entrances of villages, near the choultries on the borders of tanks, near rivers, in the market-places, and elsewhere. The Hindus also delight in placing these idols of stone under the shade of leafy trees, especially of those reputed sacred, such as the Aswattha, the Alai, the Vepu.[2] Some of these idols are placed in shrines, and others in the open air, etc.

Most Hindu temples present a very poor appearance, being more like barns or stables than buildings consecrated to the gods. Some of them are used as places of public assembly, courts of justice, or rest-houses for travellers. There are many, however, which as seen from

---

1 The ceremonies performed in honour of the infernal deities took place at sunset; and it is believed that the entrances of the temples of these divinities faced towards the west.

2 The Ficus religiosa, the Ficus indica, and the Melia azadirachta.

a distance have an imposing effect and excite the admiration of the traveller. They recall to mind those ancient times when architects had an eye for posterity as well as for their contemporaries, and were much more intent on making their works durable than on securing elegance at the cost of solidity.

The structure of the large temples, both ancient and modern, is everywhere the same. The Hindus, devoted as they are to ancestral customs, have never introduced innovations in the construction of their public edifices. **Their architectural monuments, such as they exist today, are probably better examples of building as practised by ancient civilized nations than the ruins of Egyptians and Greeks, concerning which European scholars have so much to say.**

The entrance gate of the great pagodas opens through a high, massive pyramidal tower, the summit of which is ordinarily topped by a crescent or half-moon. This gate faces the east, a position which is observed in all their temples, great and small. The pyramid or tower is called the gopuram.

Beyond the tower is a large court, at the farther end of which is another gate, opening like the first through a pyramid of the same form, but smaller; through this you pass to a second and smaller court, which is in front of the shrine containing the principal idol.

In the middle of this second court and facing the entrance to the shrine, you generally see

upon a large pedestal, or within a kind of pavilion open on all sides and supported by four pillars, a coarsely sculptured stone figure, either of a bull lying flat on its belly, or of a lingam, if the temple is dedicated to Siva; or of the monkey Hanuman, or of the serpent Capella, if it is a temple of Vishnu; or of the god Vigheshwara; or maybe of some other symbol of Hindu worship. This is the first object which the natives worship before entering the shrine itself.

The door of the shrine is generally low and narrow, and it is the only opening which allows a free passage of air and light from outside, for the use of windows is entirely unknown in the Peninsula. The interior of the shrine is habitually shrouded in darkness, or is lighted only by the feeble flicker of a lamp which burns day and night by the side of the idol. One experiences a sort of involuntary shock on entering one of these dark recesses. The interior of the shrine is generally divided into two parts, sometimes into three. The first, which may be called the nave, is the largest, and it is here that the worshippers assemble. The second is called the *adytum*, or sanctuary, where the idol to whom the shrine is consecrated is placed. This chamber is smaller and much darker than the first. It is generally kept shut, and the door can be opened only by the officiating priest, who with some of his acolytes, has alone a right to enter; its mysterious precincts for the purpose of washing and dressing the idol and presenting the offerings of the faithful, such as flowers, incense of sandalwood, lighted lamps, fruit, butter-milk, rich apparel, and jewels.

Some of the modern Hindu temples are vaulted, but most of them have flat roofs supported by several rows of massive stone pillars, the capitals of which are composed of two heayy stones crossed, on which are placed the beams, also of stone, which extend through the length and breadth of the building. The beams again are covered horizontally with slabs of stone strongly cemented to prevent leakage. Whether the object be to make these buildings more imposing and solid, or to preserve them from the danger of fire, wood is never employed except for the doors.

The *adytum,* or sanctuary, is often constructed with a dome, but the building as a whole is generally very low. The low elevation; the difficulty with which the air finds a way through a single narrow and habitually closed passage; the unhealthy odours rising from the mass of fresh and decaying flowers; the burning lamps; the oil and butter spilt in libations; the excrements of the bats that take up their abode in these dark places; finally, and above all, the fetid perspiration of a multitude of people;—all contribute to render these sacred shrines excessively unhealthy. Only a Hindu could remain for any length of time in their heated and pestilential precincts without suffocation.[1]

---

1. The Abbe nowhere remarks on the burning of camphor, which plays so conspicuous part in all Hindu worship. —Ed.

The principal idol is generally placed in a niche. It is clothed with garments more or less magnificent, and on great festivals is sometimes adorned with rare vestments and rich jewels. A crown of gold set with precious stones often adorns its head. For the most part, however, the idols of stone wear a cap like a sugar-loaf, which imparts to the whole figure the appearance of a pyramid. The Hindus, by the way, appear to have a special fancy for the form of a pyramid, which perhaps is due to some symbolical notion. We know that various nations of antiquity, among others the Egyptians, regarded the pyramid as the symbol of immortality and of life, the beginning of which was represented by the base and the end or death by the summit. The pyramid was also the emblem of fire.

In vain are Hindu idols decked with rich ornaments; they are not rendered thereby less disagreeable in appearance. Their physiognomy is generally of ugliness, which is carefully enhanced by daubing the images from time to time with a coating of dark paint. Some of the idols, thanks to the generous piety of rich votaries, have their eyes, mouth, and ears of gold or silver.

The idols exposed to public veneration in the temples are of stone, while those carried in procession through the streets are of metal, as are also the domestic gods which every Brahmin keeps and worships in his house.

It is forbidden to make idols of wood or other easily destructible material. I know only one, that of the goddess Mariamma, which is of wood. For this image the wood of a certain tree is employed, the trunk of which is red inside, and which, when cut, exudes a sap the colour of blood, a characteristic which accords well with the merciless nature of this cruel divinity. It is true, one also often sees statues of clay or of masonry, but these are not of much account.

No idol can become an object of worship until it has been duly consecrated by a number of ceremonies. It is necessary first of all that the deity should be invoked, in order that it may fix its abode in the idol, and be incorporated with it; and this must be done by a Brahmin purohit. New temples are also subjected to a solemn inauguration, and all objects destined for their service must be formally consecrated. Both temples and idols are liable to be desecrated on many occasions. If, for example, a European, a Mahomedan, or a Pariah entered a sanctuary or touched an idol, that very instant the divinity would take its departure. And in order to induce it to return, all the ceremonies would have to be begun over again, and performed more elaborately and at greater cost than before.

Besides the idols which are to be found inside every temple, the walls and four sides of the supporting pillars are covered with various figures. On the facade of the building niches are arranged, to contain symbolical

figures representing men and animals, for the most part in indecent attitudes. Furthermore, the walls of the temple enclosure, which are no less thick and solid than the actual buildings, are also sometimes covered with these images. Outside the shrine, opposite and close to the entrance door, and sometimes in the middle of one of the courts, there is commonly seen a granite pillar, from forty to fifty feet high, octagonal in shape, and square at the base of the shaft; on each side of the lower part figures are sculptured. The pedestal is a solid mass of hewn stone. The capital of the column ends in a square cornice, at the four angles of which small bells are usually suspended. Above this, again, is a chafing dish in which incense is burned at certain times, or else lighted lamps are placed there.

The traveller often sees on the roads, and even in remote spots, lofty columns of this kind, on which certain devotees place lamps from time to time. During the feast of Deepavali, lamps are to be seen burning every evening on such columns. Sometimes the pillars are wreathed with pieces of new cloth, which are finally set on fire. These details favour the view that the pillars, constructed as they always are in places exposed to the east, are consecrated to the sun or to the element of fire.

Temple offices are held by persons of various castes. Nevertheless, all posts of any importance, and especially those which confer profit and dignity, are always held by Brahmins.

Among the numerous officials in Hindu worship the sacrificers occupy first rank; then come the consultative committees, the directors of ceremonies, the collectors of temple revenues, and the treasurers. Besides these, there are hosts of subordinates who assist in the administration of the temple funds, and in the supervision and direction of religious observances.

Sometimes, but not frequently, the high functions of sacrificers are performed by common Sudras and even Pariahs. At one of the most famous temples of Mysore, called Melkota, during the great festival which is there celebrated annually, the Pariahs are the first to enter the sanctuary and to offer sacrifices to the idol, and it is only after they have finished that the Brahmins begin their sacrifices.

A fact worthy of remark is that the officiating priests wear no special costume in the exercise of their sacerdotal functions; they are dressed in their ordinary clothes, which are, however, newly washed for the purpose.

In most of the temples the oblations and sacrifices are confined to the simple products of nature. The offering of lamps is also specially in vogue. Sometimes thousands may be seen burning around the idol and in the enclosure of the temple; they are filled with butter, which is a much more acceptable offering to the gods than oil.

Hindu priests offer up sacrifices regularly twice a day, morning and evening. The idol to

which the sacrifice is offered is first thoroughly washed, and the water used for this purpose is brought from the river with much pomp and ceremony. In some of the great pagodas it is brought on the backs of elephants, preceded by dancing-girls and musicians, and escorted by a great number of Brahmins and various attendants. In other temples the Brahmins themselves go with a similar show of, ceremony to fetch the water morning and evening, bringing it on their heads in large brass vessels. The water that remains after the idol has been washed is called *tirtham*, holy water.

As soon as the task of washing the idol is over, the priest performs its toilet, which consists in putting on its clothes and tracing on its forehead one of the signs which the Hindus are accustomed to wear on their own foreheads. Puja is then offered to it. During these ceremonies the officiating priest tinkles a little bell, which is held in his left hand, the object no doubt being to call the attention of the worshippers to each stage in the ceremonial which is taking place inside the shrine and out of sight.

After completing his mysterious duties, which must be concealed from profane eyes[1]: the priest appears and distributes to the people who are assembled in the hall of the temple

1. In Vishnu temples these 'mysterious duties' are performed behind a curtain drawn between the worshippers and the idol. —Ed.

fragments of the offerings made to the idol. This *prasada* (sacred gift) is received with eagerness. If it is fruit or some other nutritious substance, it is eaten; if it is flowers, the men stick them in their turbans, while the women entwine them in their hair. Last of all, the priest pours into the hollow of each person's hand a little *tirtham,* which is drunk immediately. After this all the worshippers retire.

The courtesans or dancing-girls attached to each temple take their place in the second rank; they are called Devadasis servants of the gods, but the public call them by the name of prostitutes. And in fact they are bound by their profession to grant their favours, if such they be, to anybody demanding them in return for ready money. It appears that at first they were reserved exclusively for the enjoyment of the Brahmins. And these lewd women, who make a public traffic of their charms, are consecrated in a special manner to the worship of the divinities of India. Every temple of any importance has in its service a band of eight, twelve, or more. Their official duties consist in dancing and singing within the temple twice a day, morning and evening, and also at all public ceremonies. The first they execute with sufficient grace, although their attitudes are lascivious and their gestures indecorous. As regards their singing, it is almost always confined to verses describing some licentious episode in the history of their gods. These women are also present at marriages and other solemn family meetings. They are brought up

in this licentiousness from infancy, and are recruited from various castes, some among them belonging to respectable families. It is not unusual for pregnant women, with the object of obtaining a safe delivery, to make a vow, with the consent of their husbands, to devote the child that they carry in their womb, if it should turn out a girl, to the temple service. In fact no shame whatever to parents is attached whose daughters adopt this career.

The courtesans are the only women in India who enjoy the privilege of learning to read, to dance, and to sing. A well-bred and respectable woman would for this reason blush to acquire anyone of these accomplishments[1].

The Devadasis receive a fixed salary for the religious duties which they perform; but as the amount is small they supplement it by selling their favours in as profitable a manner as possible. In the attainment of this object they are probably more skilful than similar women in other countries. They employ all the resources and artifices of coquetry. Perfumes, elegant costumes, coiffures best suited to set off the beauty of their hair, which they entwine with sweet-scented flowers; a profusion of jewels worn with much taste on different parts of the body; graceful and voluptuous attitudes:

1. In these days female education is slowly extending to all classes. and the prejudice which formerly existed no longer applies to women learning to read and sing, though dancing is still restricted to the professional dancing-girls. and is not considered respectable. —Ed.

such are the snares with which these sirens allure the Hindus.

Nevertheless, to the discredit of Europeans it must be confessed that the quiet seductions which Hindu prostitutes know how to exercise with so much skill, resemble in no way the disgraceful methods of the wretched beings who give themselves up to a similar profession in Europe, and whose indecent behaviour, cynical impudence, obscene and filthy words of invitation are enough to make any sensible man who is not utterly depraved shrink from them with horror. Of all the women in India it is the courtesans, and especially those attached to the temples, who are the most decently clothed. Indeed they are particularly careful not to expose any part of the body. Experience has no doubt taught them that for a woman to display her charms damps sensual ardour instead of exciting it, and that the imagination is more easily captivated than the eye.

God forbid, however, that anyone should believe me to wish to say a word in defence of the comparative modesty and reserve of the dancing-girls of India! Actions can only be judged by their motives; and certainly, if these Indian women are more reserved in public than their sisters in other countries which call themselves more civilized, the credit is due not to their innate modesty but to national prejudice. In fact, the Hindus strictly maintain an outward appearance of decency, and attach great importance to the observance of strict decorum in public. The most shameless

prostitute would never dare to stop a man in the streets; and she in her turn would indignantly repulse any man who ventured to take any indecent liberty with her. The man who behaved familiarly with one of these women in public would be censured and despised by everybody who witnessed the scandal. Is it the same among ourselves?

After the dancing-girls come the players of musical instruments attached to the service of the temples. Every pagoda of any importance always has a more or less numerous band of them. They, as well as the dancing-girls, are obliged to attend the temple twice a day, and to fill it with sounds. Their presence at all feasts and ceremonies is likewise obligatory. Moreover, they cannot be dispensed with during the great family feasts and ceremonies. **The Hindu taste for music is so marked that there is not a single gathering, however small, which has not some musicians at its head.**

Those who are regularly attached to a pagoda receive a fixed salary. The instruments on which they play are for the most part clarionets and trumpets; they have also cymbals and several kinds of small drums. The Hindus recognise a kind of harmony, however, in two parts: they have always a bass and a high counter-tenor or alto. The latter is produced by a wind instrument in the form of a tube widened at its base, the sounds of which have some resemblance to those of the bagpipe.

The vocal part is executed by a second band of musicians, who take turns with the dancing-girls in singing hymns in honour of the gods. Sometimes the Brahmins and other worshippers form the chorus, or sing separately sacred poems of their own composition.

The Nattuva, or conductor, is the most remarkable of all the musicians. In beating time he taps with his fingers on a narrow drum. As he beats, his head, shoulders, arms, thighs, and in fact all the parts of his body perform successive movements; and simultaneously he utters inarticulate cries, thus animating the musicians both by voice and gesture. At - times one would think he was agitated by violent convulsions.

The dancing-women, the chorus, and the orchestra take turn and turn about during a religious ceremony, which often terminates with a procession round the temple.

Morning and evening the courtesans before leaving never fail to perform for the idol, singing the while, the ceremony of the *arati*, for the purpose of averting the fatal influence caused by the looks of evil-minded persons, an influence from which the gods themselves are not exempt.

The whole musical repertoire of the Hindus is reduced to thirty-six airs, which are called ragas; but most of the musicians hardly know half of them.

Hindu music, whether vocal or instrumental, may be pleasing to the natives, but I do not think it can give the slightest pleasure to anyone else, however little sensitive be his ear. Hindu musicians learn to play and sing methodically; they keep excellent time; and they have, as we have, a variety of keys. In spite of all this, their songs have always appeared to me uninspiring and monotonous.

We must remember that Hindu music at the present day is the same as it has always been; and that, as in the case of their other arts, it has undergone no alteration and has not been improved in any way. We shall then feel obliged to be more indulgent; indeed, we may even feel astonished that Hindu music attained such perfection at the very beginning. For it is almost certain that the scale used at present by the Hindus has existed from the earliest times. It bears moreover a striking resemblance to ours, being composed of the same number of notes, arranged in the same way, as follows:

Sa ri ga ma pa da ni sa
Do re mi fa sol la si do.

There is nothing into which the Hindus do not introduce some superstitious notion, and it would have been a miracle if music—a diversion of the gods themselves—had not furnished them with means of satisfying their taste in this direction. Every note of the Hindu scale has a marked characteristic of some divinity, and includes several hidden meanings deduced from its particular sound or from something similar to it. There are also notes

expressing joy, sadness, sweetness, anger, etc. And Hindu musicians take great care not to confound notes intended to express these varying passions of the human soul.

All the musicians who play wind instruments are taken from the low barber caste, the profession being handed down from father to son.

Worship in the country being very expensive, the priests and servants of the temples have, necessarily, various sources of unfailing revenue. In some districts a kind of tithe is collected out of the whole produce of the harvest; in others, every temple has in its absolute possession extensive lands which are exempt from all taxation, and the produce of which is exclusively assigned to the maintenance of the temple and of its numerous staff. I have mentioned that in the case of these persons perquisites are of no small importance. The offerings of rich devotees, which are divided among them in proportion to their rank and dignity, are sometimes so considerable, in the principal temples, that they have aroused the cupidity of the princes of the country, particularly of Mahomedans. These latter, as a sort of compensation for tolerating a religion which they abhorred, thought fit to take possession of more than half of these offerings.

There is no trick which the Brahmins will not employ in order to excite the fervour of the worshippers, and thus to enrich themselves by their offerings. The most obvious means generally produce the best results. In the

foremost rank we must place the oracles, a rich mine of wealth which pagan priests of other countries worked long ago with great success, and which the lapse of ages has not yet exhausted for the priests of India. Here it is the idol itself which addresses the profoundly attentive crowd of worshippers, who are unable to understand that some cunning person concealed inside or close by the god of stone, is speaking through the mouth of the idol. The idol, or its interpreter, also undertakes to foretell the future; but these oracles, like those of ancient Greece, contain some ambiguous or double meaning. Consequently, whatever the issue may be, the Brahmins always find some way of making it agree, with their predictions[1].

If the flow of offerings by any chance decreases, the idol will inveigh vehemently against the indifference and meanness of the inhabitants of the district, proclaiming once for all that if this state of things continues, it will withdraw its protection from them and will even resort to the expedient of decamping in search of other more grateful, and especially more and generous worshippers[1].

Or perhaps the devout mob will some day find the hands and feet of their cherished idol bound with chains. Cruel creditors, it is announced, have brought it to this humiliating condition because it could not pay certain

---

1. These false oracles are confined to temples dedicated to the inferior deities.—Ed.

sums of money which it had borrowed in times of need; and they have sworn not to restore it to liberty until the whole sum, capital and interest, which is due to them shall have been repaid. Touched with compassion, the devotees will hasten to consult together and exact contributions from all possible sources until the sum necessary to liquidate the liabilities of their deity has been furnished to the Brahmins. As soon as the money is secured, the chains of the idol will fall off, to the great satisfaction of everybody. In some famous temples, such as that of Tirupati, they use silver instead of iron chains to bind the sacred limbs of the idol.

There is another expedient to which the Brahmins frequently have recourse. All of a sudden it is proclaimed abroad that the idol has been attacked by a dangerous disease caused by the grief it experiences on seeing the devotion of the people abating from day to day.[1] The idol is taken down from its pedestal and carried to the entrance of the temple, where it is exposed to the public gaze. Its head and temples are rubbed with sundry lotions; drugs and medicines are placed before it; the priests from time to time feel its pulse with display of the gravest uneasiness. Still the symptoms of the disease develop from day to day and the priests begin to despair of the recovery of the idol. This alarming intelligence

1. This remark also applies only to the temples dedicated to the inferior deities.—Ed.

is bruited abroad, and presents and offerings soon arrive from all sides. At sight of these the idol's strength begins to return little by little; then it becomes convalescent; and finally it is cured and restored to its place.

Fear and awe are also means which the Brahmins turn to good account in order to renew the wavering faith of the people. They engage certain confederates, into whose bodies they affirm the angry god has sent a *pisacha,* or demon, in order to avenge some outrage which it has received from wicked men. One frequently meets with charlatans who fall into dreadful convulsions and make contortions and grimaces calculated to frighten the stoutest heart. In their calmer moments they give a piteous and detailed account of their misfortunes, which they attribute to the just resentment of the god, who is punishing them for their indifference towards himself and his ministers. They gabble phrases in many dialects, asserting that it is the demon who inspires them, and who has imparted to them the gift of languages.

But this is not imputed to them as a crime; it is all laid to the charge of the devil that possesses them. The multitude are filled with fear at the sight of one of these impostors, and prostrate themselves before him, worshipping the demon who has taken up its abode in him, and offering him oblations and sacrifices, in order to propitiate him and prevent him from injuring them. The demoniac is given his fill of meat and drink; and when he departs he is accompanied with much pomp and music to the next village, where he plays the same trick and finds just as many dupes. When he is pleased to come to his senses again, he exhorts his symphathetic audience to profit by the terrible example which he affords them, to show more faith in their god than he did, and to ensure the god's favour and protection by numerous gifts and offerings.

Miracles are a most profitable branch of business for Brahmins. They have all kinds, and suitable for every disease. The blind recover their sight. The lame walk, the dead come to life again. But the most popular miracle is that which gives fecundity to women. One continually hears of women whose pious devotion has obtained for them the signal favour of bearing children. Barrenness is the greatest possible curse to a woman in India, and the most dreaded of all the misfortunes that can befall a Hindu family.

Other nations which are very proud of their enlightenment and morality suppress the natural desire of seeing oneself born again in one's numerous progeny from considerations of personal interest and ambition, and regard the fruitfulness of their women with aversion. They are, moreover, not ashamed of resorting to wicked and disgusting means of reducing or destroying it altogether, thus outraging the most holy instincts of nature in order that they may not deprive themselves of the means of satisfying their ambition or of procuring the luxuries of life, as if the love of a father for his

children were not the greatest of all pleasures. Animated in this respect by the noblest and purest sentiments, the Hindus consider a man happy in proportion to the number of children he possesses. Among them, indeed, children are considered to be the blessing of a house. However numerous a man's family may be, he never ceases to offer prayers for its Increase.

The children, it is true, soon become useful to their parents. At five or six years old they begin to tend the calves, while those a little older take care of the cows and oxen. And as soon as they are strong enough, they assist their fathers in tilling the fields or help in some other way to maintain the family.

There is a superstition, admirable enough in its way, which is a powerful factor in keeping up in the mind of a Hindu this ardent desire of seeing his race prolonged. In his eyes there is no misfortune equal to that of not leaving a son or a grandson behind to perform the last duties in connexion with his funeral. Such a deprivation is regarded as capably of preventing all access to an Abode of Bliss after death.

Hence it is that we see women who are slower in conceiving children they would wish, hastening from temple to temple, and sometimes ruining themselves in the extravagant gifts which they offer in order to obtain from the gods the inestimable favour of becoming mothers. Expert at reaping profit

from the virtues as well as the vices of their countrymen, the Brahmins see in these touching impulses of nature merely a means of gaining wealth, and also at the same time an opportunity of satisfying their carnal lusts with impunity. There are few temples where the presiding deity does not claim the power of curing barrenness in women. And there are some whose renown in this respect is unrivalled, such, for example, as that of Tirupati to which women flock in crowds to obtain children from the god Venkateswara. On their arrival, the women hasten to disclose the object of their pilgrimage to the Brahmins, the managers of the temple. The latter advise them to pass the night in the temple, where, they say, the great Venkateswara, touched by their devotion, will perhaps visit them in the spirit and accomplish that which until then has been denied to them through human power. I must draw a curtain over the sequel of this deceitful suggestion. The reader already guesses at it.

People who have not sufficiently reflected upon the extremes to which the superstitious and fanatical credulity of a people may be carried, have regarded as untrue the stories which Father Gerbillon, Tavernier, and other travellers have told of the Dalai Lama. His excrements are carefully preserved, dried, and distributed as relics to pious Tibetans, who, when they fall ill, make use of them as an internal medicine, which is considered to be a sovereign remedy for all diseases. The fact I am about to relate, which, although even more

revolting, is nevertheless quite true, will render any similar stories credible enough. It is not without shame that I enter upon an account of the disgusting incidents which I am here to describe. I would have passed them over in silence if the very nature of this work had not imposed upon me the painful duty of telling everything.

At Nanjangud, a village situated about ten leagues south of Seringapattam, there is a temple, famous throughout Mysore. Among the numerous votaries who flock to it are many women, who go to implore the help of the idol in curing their sterility. Offerings and prayers are not the only ceremonies which have to be gone through. On leaving the temple the woman, accompanied by her husband, has to go to a place where all the pilgrims are accustomed to resort to answer the calls of nature. There the husband and the wife collect with their hands a certain quantity of ordure and form it into a small pyramid, which they are careful to mark with a sign that will enable them to recognize it. Then they go to the neighbouring tank and mix in the hollow of their hands the filth which has soiled their fingers. (But I will spare my readers the rest.) After having performed their ablutions they retire. Two or three days afterwards they visit their pyramid, and, still using their hands, turn the filthy mass over and over and examine it as carefully and as seriously as the Roman augurs scrutinized the entrails of sacrificed animals, in order to see if any insects have

been engendered in it. In this case it would be a very good omen, showing that the woman would soon be pregnant. But if, after careful search, not even the smallest insect is visible, the poor couple, sad and discouraged, return home in the full conviction that the expenses they have been put to and the pains they have taken have been of no avail[1].

At Mogur, another village situated a short distance from the former, there is a small temple dedicated to Tipamma, a female divinity, in whose honour a great festival is celebrated every year. The goddess, placed in a beautifully ornamented palanquin, is carried in procession through the streets. In front of her there is another divinity, a male. These two idols, which are entirely nude, are placed in immodest postures, and by help of a piece of mechanism a disgusting movement is imparted to them as long as the procession continues. This disgusting spectacle excites transport of mirth, manifested by shouts and bursts of laughter. Nor is this all. A Pariah, who has made a special study of all the obscene and filthy expressions to be found in the Miuda language, is chosen; the goddess Tipamma is then evoked and takes up her abode in his person. Then anyone who wishes to hear foul expressions stands before the man, and he is certain to be satisfied. As it is supposed to be Tipamma who speaks through the mouth of

1. We believe that no such disgusting practice exists nowadays.—Ed.

the Pariah, the devotees, far from being offended with him, are quite pleased with the goddess for having deigned to overwhelm them with insults. Even, high-caste Hindus are to be seen at this festival seeking to obtain the coveted honour.

The goddess Tipamma of Mogur is not the only member of her family. She has six sisters, who are not in any way inferior to her in point of decency and politeness. Each one of them has her own temple, in which like ceremonies are performed. In the whole of Southern Mysore, from Alambadi as far as Wynad, for a distance of more than thirty leagues, these revels are held in the highest esteem.

There are temples in certain isolated places, too, where debauchery is the only service agreeable to the presiding deity. There children are promised to women who, laying aside all shame, grant their favours to all persons indiscriminately.

There is one of these sinks of iniquity five or six leagues from the village where I am writing these pages, on the banks of the Cauvery, in a lonely place called Junginagatta. The temple is not striking to look at, but the January feast is celebrated there with the most elements of vice. People have also told me about a temple of the same description near Kadynadai, in the district of Coimbatore, and another not far from Mududorai, in Eastern Mysore.

According to Herodotus and Strabo, every woman among the Assyrians and Babylonians

was obliged to prostitute herself once in her life in the temple of the goddess Mylitta, the Aphrodite of the Greeks. Here the scene, changes. It is no longer a question of licentious libertines profiting by the vicious tendencies or the stupid credulity of women in order to satisfy their passions. It is concerning the silly fanatics who make it their task to torture themselves and to mutilate their bodies in a hundred different ways. It is not uncommon to hear of Hindus, in case, of a serious illness or of some imminent danger, making a vow to mortify some important part of their bodies, on condition of recovery. The most common penance of this sort consists in stamping upon the shoulders, chest, and other parts of the body, with a red-hot iron, the marks symbolical of their gods—brandings which are never effaced, and which they display with as much ostentation as a warrior does the wounds he has received in battle.[1]

Devotees are often seen stretched at full length on the ground and trotting in that posture all round the temples, or, during solemn processions, before the cars which carry the idols. It is a remarkable sight to see a crowd of fanatics rolling in this manner, quite regardless of stones, thorns, and other obstacles. Others, inspired by extreme fanaticism, voluntarily throw themselves down to be crushed under the wheels of the car on which the idol is borne[1]. And the crowds that

1. This has now been prohibited by law.—Ed.

witness these acts of madness far from preventing them applaud them heartily and regard them as the very acme of devotion.

Chidimari is another torture to which devotees submit themselves in honour of the goddess Mariamma, one of the most evil-minded and bloodthirsty of all the deities of India. At many of the temples consecrated to this cruel goddess, there is a sort of gibbet erected opposite the door. At the extremity of the crosspiece, or arm, a pulley is suspended through which a cord passes with a hook at the end. The man who has made a vow to undergo this cruel penance places himself under the gibbet and a priest then beats the fleshy part of the back until it is quite benumbed. After that the hook is fixed into the flesh thus prepared and in this way the unhappy wretch is raised in the air. While suspended he is careful not to show any sign of pain; indeed he continues to laugh, jest, and gesticulate in order to amuse the spectators, who applaud and shout with laughter. After swinging in the air for the prescribed time the victim is let down again, and, as soon as his wounds are dressed, he returns home in triumph[1].

Some votaries, again, are to be met with

1. 'Hook-swinging,' as this is called, is still practised in the Madura district. Though the magistracy have orders to do all they can to prevent it, by dissuading men from offering themselves as victims, still, as it is not under ordinary circumstances a criminal offence, it cannot be prevented by legal process.—Ed.

who make a vow to walk with bare feet on burning coals. For this purpose they kindle a large pile of wood; and when the flames are extinguished and all the wood consumed, they place the glowing embers in a space about twenty feet in length. The victim stands at one extremity with his feet in a puddle expressly prepared for the purpose, takes a spring, and runs quickly over the burning embers till he reaches another puddle on the other side. In spite of these precautions very few, as one can imagine, escape from the ordeal with their feet uninjured. Others, whose weak limbs do not permit of their running over the hot embers, cover the upper part of the body with a wet cloth, and holding a chafing-dish filled with burning coals, pour the contents over their heads. This feat of devotion is called the Fire-bath.

Another kind of torture consists in piercing both cheeks and passing a wire of silver or some other metal through the two jaws between the teeth. Thus bridled, the mouth cannot be opened without acute pain. Many fanatics have been known to travel a distance of twenty miles with their jaws thus maimed, and remain several days in this state, taking only liquid nourishment, or some clear broth poured into the mouth. I have seen whole companies of them, men and women, condemned by their self-inflicted torture to enforced silence, going on a pilgrimage to some temple where this form of penance is especially recommended. There are others, again, who

pierce their nostrils or the skin of their throats in the same way.

I could not help shuddering one day at seeing one of these imbeciles with his lips pierced by two long nails, which crossed each other so that the point of one reached to the right eye and the point of the other to the left. I saw him thus disfigured at the gate of a temple consecrated to the cruel goddess Mariamma. The blood was still trickling down his chin; yet the pain he must have been enduring did not prevent him from dancing and performing every kind of buffoonery before a crowd of spectators, who showed their admiration by giving him abundant alms.

There are a great many ordinary forms of penance, which elsewhere would appear more than sufficiently painful; but devout Hindus do not rest satisfied with these; they try unceasingly to invent new methods of self-torture. Thus, for example, a fanatic self-torturer makes a vow to cut half his tongue off, executes it coolly with his own hands, puts the amputated portion in an open cocoanut shell; and offers it on his knees to the divinity.

Then, again, there are others who, apparently having nothing better to do, bind themselves to go on a pilgrimage to some distant shrine by measuring their length along the ground throughout the whole distance. Beginning at their very doors, pilgrims of this description stretch themselves on the ground, rise again, advance two steps, again lie down, again rise, and continue thus till they reach

their destination. Considering the length of their journeys and the fatigue of such exercise, it is easy to imagine that the pilgrims do not go far off the route to sleep at the end of the day. Persons have been seen attempting to measure their length in this way along the entire road which runs between the sacred town of Benares and the temple of Jagannath Puri, a distance of more than two hundred leagues. I should not like to swear, however, that they really accomplished such a feat.

This tendency of Hindus to submit their bodies to severe and often cruel tortures, or to spend their means in costly offerings, is manifested whenever they find themselves in critical circumstances, and particularly in times of sickness.

There is not a single Hindu who does not in such cases make a vow to perform something more or less onerous on condition that he is delivered safe and sound from his unfortunate predicament. The rich make vows either to celebrate solemn festivals at certain temples, or to present to the pagoda some gift, such as a cow, a buffalo, pieces of cloth or other stuffs, gold or silver ornaments, etc. If the eye, nose, ear, or any other organ be afflicted, they offer to the idols an image of it in gold or silver.

Among the numerous offerings which this superstitious mania causes to flow into the temples of the Hindu gods, there is one common enough, but which, without the perquisites which accompany it, would

contribute very little to increase the wealth of the Brahmin priests. It consists in offering one's nails and hair to some divinity. It is well known that men in India are in the habit of shaving the head and leaving only a single small tuft of hair to grow on the crown. Those who make the particular vow referred to refrain, for many years together, from cutting their nails and hair. Then at a certain fixed time, they proceed in state to the temple, and there, with great ceremony, get rid of the superfluous growth of hair and nails, which they lay at the feet of the divinity whom they wish to honour. This custom is practised only by men; it is chiefly recommended to those who believe themselves to be possessed with a devil[1].

We must do justice to the Brahmins by remarking that they are never so silly as to impose on themselves vows of self-torture. They leave these pious pastimes to the Sudras. And even the Sudras who practise such penances are for the most part men of low birth who do so to gain their livelihood; or else fanatical sectaries of Siva or Vishnu, actuated by religious mania, or more often by an inordinate desire of securing the applause and admiration of the public.

Apart from ordinary superstitious practices which nourish everywhere, there are certain temples which, in this respect, enjoy special privileges; such, for example, as that of Tirupati

1. This custom is also practised among Sudra women.—Ed.

in the south of the country. This temple, is dedicated to Vishnu under the name of Venkateswara. Immense multitudes of pilgrims flock to it from all parts of India, bringing offerings of all sorts, in food, stuffs, gold, silver, jewels, costly cloths, horses, cows, etc. which are so considerable that they suffice to maintain several thousands of persons employed in the various offices of worship, which is there conducted with extraordinary magnificence.

Among the noticeable peculiarities which distinguish the great feasts of this temple there is one which I must not pass over in silence. At a certain time of the year a grand procession is formed, which attracts an immense crowd of persons of both sexes. While the image of Venkateswara is borne through the streets on a magnificent car, the Brahmins who preside at the ceremony, go about among the crowd and select the most beautiful women they can find, demanding them of their husbands or parents in the name of Venkateswara, for whose service, it is asserted, they are destined of his priests[1].

It is thus that the seraglio of Tirupati is recruited. When the god takes it into his head that some of his wives are beginning to grow old or are no longer pleasing to him, he signifies through the priests his intention of divorcing them. A mark is branded on their thighs or

1. Such proceedings would hardly be tolerated in the present day.—Ed.

breasts with a red-hot iron, representing the god Venkateswara, and they receive a certificate showing that they have faithfully served a certain number of years as legitimate wives of the god, and are therefore recommended to the charitable public. Then they are dismissed, and provided with their certificate of good conduct they go about the country under the name of Kali-yuga-Lakshmis (the Lakshmis[1] of Kali-yuga). Wherever they go their wants are abundantly supplied.

This system of procuring wives to their idols is not a peculiarity of the temple of Tirupati. The priests of many other temples have found it convenient to have recourse to it, as for instance those in charge of the temple of Jagannath, which is even more famous than the temple of Tirupati. Religious ceremonies are conducted in this temple: with the greatest magnificence. It is situated near the sea on the coast of Orissa. The principal divinity worshipped there is represented under a monstrous shape without arms or head. What particularly distinguishes this pagoda is that it is a centre of union among ,the Hindus. Although it is specially consecrated to Vishnu, there are no distinctions between sects and castes.

Everybody is admitted, and may offer worship in his own way to the presiding deity. Accordingly, pilgrims resort thither from all

1. Lakshmi is the name of the wife of Vishnu.

parts of India; the disciples of Vishnu and of Siva frequenting it with equal zeal. The Bairagis and the Gosais from the North, the Dasarus and the Jangamas from the South, lay aside their mutual animosities when they approach this sacred place, and it is, along with Tiruspati, perhaps the only spot in India where they do so[1]. While sojourning there they seem to form but one brotherhood. It is at this temple especially that one sees the religious fanatics, of whom I have already spoken above, throwing themselves before the car of the idol and allowing themselves to be crushed beneath its wheels.

Several thousands of persons, chiefly Brahmins, are employed in the performance of the religious ceremonies of the temple. The crowd of pilgrims never abates. Those from the South who go on a pilgrimage to Kasi, or Benares, always take the Jagannath Puri road up the coast in order to offer en route their respectful homage to its presiding deity. Those from the North who go to the temple of Rameswaram, which is situated on a small island, also take this road.

I have made mention elsewhere of a tank or reservoir of sacred water which is found at Kumbakonam in Tanjore, and which possesses the virtue once in every twelve years of

---

1. Tirupati is the same in this respect.—Ed.

purifying all those who bathe in it from all spiritual and corporal infirmities and from all sins committed during many generations. When the time for this easy means of absolution draws nigh, an almost incredible number of pilp-rims flock to the spot from all parts of India.

At Palni, in Madura, there is a famous temple consecrated to the god Velayudha, whose devotees bring offerings of a peculiar kind, namely, large sandals beautifully ornamented and similar in shape to those worn by the Hindus on their feet. The god is addicted to hunting, and these shoes are intended for his use when he traverses the jungles and deserts in pursuit of his favourite sport. Such gifts, one might think, would go very little way towards filling the coffers of the priests of Velayudha. Nothing of the sort; Brahmins always know how to reap profit from anything. Accordingly, the new sandals are rubbed on the ground and rolled a little in the dust, and are exposed to the eyes of the pilgrims who visit the temple. It is clear enough that the sandals must have been worn on the divine feet of Velayudha; and they become the property of whosoever pays the highest.

I must add a few words concerning the religious processions of the Hindus, which in their eyes are a matter of no small importance. There is not a single temple of any note which

has not one or two processions every year. On such occasions the idols are placed on huge massive cars supported on four large solid wheels, not made, like our wheels, with spokes. etc. A big beam serves as the axle, and supports the car proper, which is sometimes fifty feet in height. The thick blocks which form the base are carved with images of men and women in the most indecent attitudes. Several stages of carved planking are raised upon this basement, gradually diminishing in width until the whole fabric has the form of a pyramid.

On the days of procession the car is adorned with coloured calicoes, costly cloths, green foliage, garlands of flowers, etc., The idol, clothed in the richest apparel and adorned with is most precious jewels, is placed in the middle of the car, beneath an elegant canopy. Thick cables are attached to the car, and sometimes more than a thousand persons are harnessed to it. A party of dancing-girls are seated on the car and surround the idol. Some of them fan the idol with fans made of peacocks' feathers; others wave yak tails gracefully from side to side. Many other persons are also mounted on the car for the purpose of directing its movements and inciting the multitude that drags it to continued efforts. All this is done in the midst of tremendous tumult and confusion.

The procession advances slowly. From time to time a halt is made, during which uproar of

shouts and cries and whistlings is kept up. The courtesans, who are present in great numbers on these solemn occasions, perform dances; while, as long as the procession continues, the drums, trumpets, and all sorts of musical instruments give forth their sounds. On one side sham combatants armed with naked sabres are to be seen fencing with one another; on another side, one sees men dancing in groups and beating time with small sticks; and somewhere else people are seen wrestling. Finally, a great number of devotees crawl slowly before the car on hands and knees. Those who have nothing else to do, shriek and shout so that even the thunder of the great Indra striking the giants would not be heard by them. But in order to form a proper idea of the terrible uproar and confusion that reigns among this crowd one must witness such a scene.

The real good which the Hindu religion does is to unite in one body under its banner the various castes and tribes of India, the differences between which are such as would otherwise constitute them, so to speak, different nations. Without this common tie it may reasonably be presumed that only disorder and anarchy would prevail.

It is quite true, therefore, that a religion, however bad and absurd it may be, is still preferable to the absence of any religion at all. Unquestionably, in my opinion, the worshipper of the Trimurti is much less contemptible than the free-thinker who presumes to deny the existence of God. **A Hindu who professes the doctrine of metempsychosis proves that he has infinitely more common sense than those vain philosophers who utilize all their logic in proving that they are merely brute beasts, and that 'death is merely an eternal sleep' for the reasoning man as well as for the animal which cannot reason.**

11

Hindu Festivals

The eleventh day of the moon is religiously observed, not only by Brahmins, but by all those castes which have the right to wear the triple cord. They keep a strict fast on this day, abstain entirely from rice, do no servile work, and give themselves up wholly to devotional exercises. The following is what the Vishnu-purana says on the subject:

Ekadasi

'The Ekadasi is a day specially set apart for the worship of Vishnu; those who offer him puja on this day ensure for themselves immortality. Even before the creation of the world the "Man of Sin" was created by Vishnu to punish mankind. He is of enormous stature, with a terrific countenance and a body absolutely black; his eyes are wild and glaring with rage; he is the executioner of mankind. Krishna, having seen this "Man of Sin," became thoughtful and pensive. Touched by the woes with which mankind was overwhelmed, Krishna resolved to remedy the evil. With this end in view he mounted the bird Garuda, son

of Vinata, and went in search of Yama, the King of Hell. The Child of the Sun, delighted at this visit of Narayana, who was master and guru of the world, hastened to offer him puja, and placed him on a massive throne of gold. No sooner had Krishna seated himself thereon than he heard the most piteous and plaintive cries. Moved with compassion, he asked the King of Naraka whence these lamentations proceeded, and what caused them.

'"The lamentations that you hear, O Lord of the World," replied Yama, "are the tears and groans of the unfortunate beings who, having spent their whole lives in sin, are now suffering the tortures of Hell, where they are treated according to their deserts."

"'Then, "said Krishna," let us go to this place of torment, that I may see for myself what these sinners are enduring."

'And he did see, and his heart was softened.

"'What!" cried he, overcome with grief, "is it possible that men, who are creatures and children of mine, are enduring such cruel agony! Shall I be a witness of their sufferings and do nothing to help them? Cannot I give them some means of avoiding them in the future?'"

'Thereupon he considered how he might bring the reign of the "Man of Sin" to an end, he being the sole cause of all mankind's misfortune. Accordingly, to preserve henceforth the human race from the torments of Naraka, he transformed himself into the Ekadasi, or eleventh day of the moon. This is, therefore, the blessed day that Vishnu has

selected in his mercy to redeem and save mankind. It is the happy day that procures the pardon of one's sins; it is the day of days, since one must look upon it as being Krishna himself.

'The inhabitants of Hell, full of gratitude for the kindness that Vishnu had showed towards them, worshipped him and chanted his praises loudly. Thereupon Vishnu, being much pleased by their prayers and praises, wished to give them an immediate proof of his goodness. Turning to the "Man of Sin," he addressed him in the following words:

'"Begone, wretched being, begone! Thy reign is over. Till now thou has been the tormentor of mankind; I command thee to let them live in peace for the future. They are my children, and I desire them to be happy. I wish, nevertheless, to assign to thee a place where thou mayest live, but thy place shall be unique; it shall be here. The Ekadasi, or eleventh day of the moon, is myself in another form. It is the day that I have chosen, in my mercy, to save men and deliver them from their sins. Nevertheless, in order that they may be worthy of so great a favour, I expressly forbid them to eat rice on this day. I ordain that thou shalt dwell in this rice. This is the abode that I assign to thee. Whoever shall have the temerity to eat this food, thus defiled by thy presence, will incorporate thee with himself, and will forfeit all hope of pardon."

'Thus spake Vishnu; and the following is the sentence of life and death which he pronounced, and which cannot be too strongly impressed on the attention of mankind:

"'I repeat, therefore, again, because I cannot say it too often: Do not eat rice on that day; whoever you are, be your position and condition what they may, do not eat rice. Once more I say, do not eat rice.'"

To fast on this holy day and to offer puja to Vishnu is to ensure the forgiveness of sins and the gratification of all one's wishes. Moreover, these further observances must be followed. On the tenth day the Sandhya must be performed, and only one meal must be eaten, and that without salt or any kind of peas or vegetables. It must only be seasoned with a small quantity of melted butter, and it must be eaten quickly. In the evening one must visit a temple dedicated to Vishnu, and, holding some darbha grass in one's hands, must meditate for some time on the greatness of the deity, addressing to him the following prayer:

'Behold me in thy presence, great god! I prostrate myself at thy feet. Hold out a helping hand to me and remove the obstacles which I encounter at each step. My feeble will is often led astray by the passions that influence me. Thou alone canst give it strength to resist such weaknesses, and keep it straight in the path of virtue.'

This prayer being ended, some darbha grass must be offered to Narayana, and the

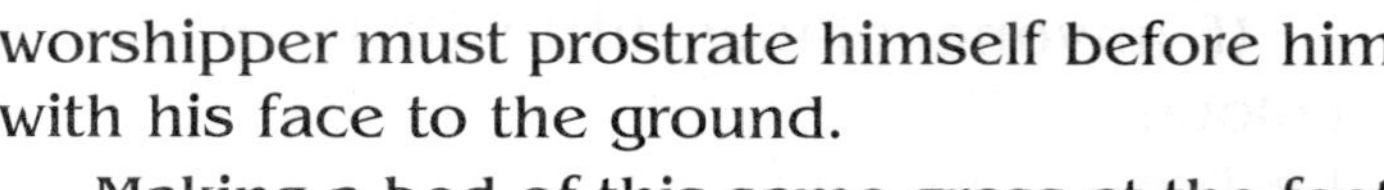

worshipper must prostrate himself before him with his face to the ground.

Making a bed of this same grass at the feet of Vishnu, he must pass the night upon it. On rising in the morning he must wash his mouth out twelve times and perform the usual ablutions. During the day he must fulfil his ordinary religious duties, the chief of which is the sacrifice to Vishnu. He must fast for the whole of the day, eating and drinking nothing. The night of the eleventh day must also be spent in a temple dedicated to Vishnu. The whole family—father, mother, wife, brothers, and children—must remain together in the presence of Vishnu, and remain awake.

The wife who performs this act of devotion along with her husband will, on her reincarnation, have a husband who will make her very happy, and by whom she will have a numerous family. Alter her death she will be conveyed to Vaikuntha, and be reunited to her first husband.

Whoever during this night shall occupy himself in drawing the emblems of the Chakra and Sankha, which Vishnu carries in his hand, will obtain the remission of his sins committed in former generations. Whoever shall make a model of these two weapons with dough of rice flour, in several colours, shall receive a much greater reward, for his sons and his grandsons shall enjoy prosperity on earth, and occnpy after their death a high place in Vaikuntha.

If anyone places little flags of various colours in Vishnu's temple he will eventually be born again king of a fine country. And if anyone allows the cloths and flags that have been offered to Vishnu to flutter freely in the wind, he will receive pardon for all his sins, however heinous they may have been. Anyone who places an umbrella over Vishnu's head will be reborn rich and powerful, and will himself have the right to use one.

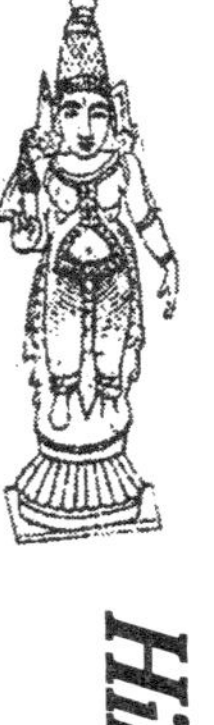

To employ oneself during this same night in making a little house of flowers for Vishnu is as meritorious a work as if one had sacrificed a horse a hundred times over. And if anyone should make this house in cloth, he will himself have a house of bricks in Vaikuntha.

On the Salagrama stone or on the image of Vishnu must then be poured some Pancha-amrita, that is to say, milk, melted butter, curds, honey, and sugar mixed together. The image must then be adorned with rich stuffs and precious jewels, and a fan must be placed before it. Having performed the *samkalpa*, and purified by the santi-yoga the five elements of which man is composed, the worshippers must fix their thoughts on Vishnu, and, holding flowers in their hands, must meditate for some time on the perfections of the deity. They must picture him to themselves in their mind's eye as seated on golden throne with his daughter by his side, casting around the effulgent light that encircles him, having sometimes two and sometimes four arms. To this Supreme Lord

of the Universe must their homage be addressed.

This act of meditation ended, the worshippers must offer him puja, beginning with the Swagata; that is to say, they must ask the god whether he is in good health, and has accomplis-hed his journey safely.

They will then present to him water to wash his feet, and to refresh him after the fatigues of his journey. They must say: 'God of Gods, receive this water to wash your feet; it is pure and sweet, and will refresh you, and it will remove the dust which has covered you on your way.'

They will then give him water for rinsing out his mouth, and more water and flowers to put on his head; some milk, honey, and sugar, mixed together, to quench his thirst; and various kinds of food to satisfy his appetite. It is thus, at intervals of three hours, that they must offer puja to Vishnu. Everything that is offered to him must be the very best that can be procured.

I have already said that they must pass the night without closing an eye for a moment; they must spend it in dancing and singing to the sound of musical instruments. It is sufficient to repeat Vishnu's names, or even to hear them repeated, to obtain the remission of all one's sins and the accomplishment of all one's desires. It is considered a meritorious action even to go and look at persons who are spending the night in the performance of these pious exercises.

Great care must be taken on this holy day not to speak to anyone who is not a true worshipper of Vishnu. To address even one word to unbelievers would cause Vishnu's worshippers to lose all the benefit of their devotion.

He who on this day hears the sound of musical instruments played in honour of Vishnu and is not enchanted, is like a dog when it hears the vina. The pious man should delight in listening to a symphony which is in itself capable of remitting sins, because it adds to the glory of the Lord of the world. He should join in the saintly throng of worshippers, when they with one accord hasten to show their devotion and their zeal by their dances, songs, and hymns in honour of the great deity.

He who objects to such acts of worship is the greatest of sinners. He who, while not actually disapproving, refrains from taking part in them, and occupies himself instead with other matters, will be punished for his indifference by being reborn as a cook in another life. He will be reborn dumb if he does not contribute as much as eyer he can towards the pomp and ceremony of the Ekadasi.

Every kind of musical instrument must be played on that night, and in fact everything that is possible must be done to contribute to Vishnu's pleasure. The worshippers must walk round the image of the god several times in procession; they must prostrate themselves before it, and from time to time they must pour milk upon its head. Each worshipper, at the conclusion of the ceremony, must give a

present to the Brahmins in proportion to his means.

Those who fast on the eleventh day break their fast before sunrise on the twelfth day. Those who faithfully observe the fast of the Ekadasi in the manner described will make sure of salvation. If anyone has killed a Brahmin or a cow, taken away the wife or property of another, committed fornication with the wife of his guru, drunk intoxicating liquors, caused abortion in a pregnant woman; all these and other similar sins, no matter how numerous or heinous they may be, will be entirely absolved by the fast of the Ekadasi, and by sacrifices offered to Vishnu on that day. Such, in brief, is what Markandeya teaches us.

Before leaving this subject I ought to mention that the precepts contained in these instructions are not strictly kept, except by a very small number of devotees. The Ekadasi, it is true, is kept as a holy day by Brahmins, and by all persons who have the right to wear the triple cord, and even by a few Sudras of good position, but they content themselves with spending the day in performing a few religious rites and in amusements. Nevertheless, they all abstain from eating rice. Towards evening, however, they have a meal composed of cakes and fruit, which greatly modifies and simplifies the severity and length of the fast prescribed by the Vishnu-purana.

Siva-Ratri

The feast of Siva-Ratri is celebrated with great ceremony, especially by the Saivaites. This is what we read in the Skanda-purana on the subject:

There is in Jambudwipa a large town known by the name of Varanasi, where dwelt a man belonging to the boya or huntsman caste, who was short of stature, very dark in complexion, and of a most violent and passionate temper. One day when out hunting in the woods, as was his wont, he killed such an enormous quantity of birds of all kinds that he was hardly able to carry them, and was obliged to sit down and rest at almost every step. Dusk was coming on while he was still in the middle of a thick forest, and anxious not to lose the spoil of his day's hunting or to become a prey to the wild beasts that infested the place, he went up to a bilva-tree, hung his game upon one of the branches, and climbed up into the tree, intending to spend the night there.

Now that night happened to be the night of the new moon of the month of Phalguna (March), a time of year when dew falls heavily and the nights are chilly. The hunter, benumbed with cold, tormented by hunger for he had eaten nothing during the day, and half dead with terror, passed a very miserable night. At the foot of the tree was a lingam, and this circumstance proved to be the salvation of the hunter. The discomforts that he was enduring

obliged him to change his position frequently, and the shaking of the branches of the Vepu caused some drops of dew, together with some leaves, flowers, and fruit, to fall on the lingarn. This fortunate accident was sufficient to win Siva's favour and to obtain for the hunter absolution for all his sins. For Siva, to whose worship this night was specially onsecrated, was much gratified at the offering thus made to his adored symbol; and he ordained that he who had made it, involuntary though his offering was, should be rewarded, and that his long fast and attendant anxieties should be reckoned in his favour.

The hunter regained his house the following morning, and died a few days afterwards. Yama, King of Hell, on hearing of his death, immediately sent his emissaries to secure him and bring him away. But Siva, on hearing of this, also sent his own emissaries to oppose those of Yama and to claim the dead man. Yama's messengers declined to yield, and a violent quarrel ensued between them and the emissaries of Siva. From insults they quickly proceeded to violence. Siva's party, being the stronger, put the agents of Naraka to flight, after severely punishing them. The latter, in shame and bitterness, went and told their story to their master, and to excite his wrath showed him the wounds that they had received in the combat.

Yama, beside himself with indignation, went at once to Kailasa to make complaint to Siva in person. At the gate of the deity's palace he found Nandi, the prime minister, to whom he explained the object of his visit, at the same time expressing his surprise that Siva should thus declare himself the protector of a common boya, a hardened sinner, whose trade necessitated the slaughter of many living creatures.

'King of Hell,' replied Nandi, 'it is true that this man has been a great sinner and that he has not scrupled to shed blood; but before he died, he, fortunately for himself, fasted, watched, and offered a sacrifice to the lingam during the night consecrated to Siva. This meritorious action has obtained for him the remission of all his sins, the protection of Siva, and an honourable place in Kailasa.'

When Yama heard Nandi's words, he became thoughtful, and withdrew without uttering another word.

This is the origin of the feast of Siva-Ratri, or Night of Siva. In commemoration of the fortunate boya the devotees of Siva spend the night and the preceding day in fasting and without sleep, entirely absorbed in worshipping the god, in offering him sacrifices, and presenting him with the bitter leaves of the bilva tree as Naivedya, which they afterwards eat.

12

Hindu Feasts

Each district and each temple even of the least importance has its own particular feasts, recurring at intervals during the course of the year; and besides these local feasts, there are many others that are generally observed everywhere, taking place at fixed periods. Feast-days are given up to rejoicings and diversions of all kinds; work is entirely suspended; relatives and friends meet together and feast each other in turn; the houses are decorated, the best jewels and apparel are worn, and the time is spent in games, which for the most part are very artless and innocent. Family feasts, however, have not the smallest resemblance to those celebrated in temples, to which the people flock from every side.

There are in all eighteen obligatory Hindu feasts in the year, but I will mention only the principal ones. First, there is the feast which is celebrated on the first day of the year, called **Ugadi,**[1] and which falls on the day of the new

---

1. This is the name given to the Telugu New Year's Day. — Ed.

moon in the month of March. On this occasion Hindus are expected to pay each other visits of ceremony. The feast lasts for three days, during which they give themselves up to enjoyment. Fireworks are let off, and cannon, rockets, and guns are heard on every side. It is about this time, also, that the officers of Government prepare their revenue accounts for the year, and that the cultivators renew the leases of the lands which they farm.

At the time of the new moon in the month of February the Lingayats, or followers of Siva, celebrate with great pomp their feast **Siva-Ratri.** This lasts three days, and during the course of it the Lingayats wash and purify their lingam, cover it with a new cloth, and offer to it sacrifices of a special character. They also visit their jangamas or gurus, and present them with gifts.

The festival of **Gauri** takes place at the time of the new moon in the month of September, and lasts many days. Gauri is another name for Parvati, the wife of Siva, who is the object of peculiar worship on this occasion. On the last day of the feast they mould a figure of the goddess in rice dough; this is placed in a shrine beautifully adorned, and is then carried with great pomp through the streets. The Gauri feast, however, is also specially dedicated to the household gods, which are represented by the implements, tools, and utensils in common use amongst the people. Thus, the farmer

collects his ploughs, his spades, and his sickles, and places them in a heap on a spot carefully purified by a layer of cow-dung. He prostrates himself at full length before the various implements of husbandry, and offers them puja and Naivedya according to the usual manner. He then puts them back in their places. The mason offers similar homage to his trowel, his square, etc., the carpenter to his axe, his saw, and his plane; the barber to his razor; the writer to his pen or stilus; the tailor to his scissors and needles; the huntsman to his gun; the fisherman to his nets; the weaver to his loom; the butcher to his cleaver; and so on in the case of all artisans.

The women, too, collect their baskets, winnows, rice-mills—in short, all their household implements, and prostrate themselves before them, offering them homage in like manner. In a word, there is not a person who, during this solemn time, does not regard as so many deities the instruments with which he gains his livelihood. The prayers which are addressed and the honours which are paid to them are intended to persuade them to continue to be useful to their possessors. In fact, the whole ceremony is based on the Hindu principle —that it is necessary to pay honour to everything which may be either useful or hurtful.

A month later, at the new moon of October, comes the feast of **Maha-navami**, known also under the name of **Dasara**, speciklly dedicated

to the memory of ancestors. This feast is considered to be so obligatory that it has become a proverb that anybody who has not the means of celebrating it should sell one of his children in order to do so. Each family offers the usual sacrifices to its deceased ancestors, and also presents them with new cloths such as are usually worn by men and women, in order that they may be properly clothed. The feast lasts nine days.

This is also the special festival of universities and schools. The students, dressed in gay apparel, parade through the streets every day, singing verses composed by their professors, who march at their head. They also recite these verses before the doors of their relatives and the principal inhabitants of the place. At the same time they dance and play in a simple fashion, marking time by striking sticks together. At the end of it all the professors receive small presents of money from the people before whom their students have performed. A portion of the sum collected is given to the students for a feast on the last day of the ceremonies, and the remainder the professors keep for themselves.

The Dasara is likewise the soldiers' feast. Princes and soldiers offer the most solemn sacrifices to the arms which are made use of in battle. Collecting all their weapons together, they call a Brahmin purohit, who sprinkles them with *tirtham,* holy water, and converts them into so many divinities by virtue of his mantras. He then makes puja to them and retires.

Thereupon, amidst the beat of drums, the blare of trumpets and other instruments, a ram is brought in with much pomp and sacrificed in honour of the various weapons of destruction. This ceremony is observed with the greatest solemnity throughout the whole South, not only by the Hindu princes and soldiers, but also by the Mahomedans, who have unreservedly adopted this practice of the Hindus. It is known by the special name of Ayudha-puja (sacrifice to arms), and is entirely military; no native belonging to the profession of arms, makes any scruple of joining in it.

In order to increase the solemnity of the feast, the princes are in the habit of giving public entertainments, to which immense crowds of people resort. These entertainments resemble very much the gladiatorial combats of the ancient Romans, consisting as they do of contests between animals or between animals. and men, and above all, between men. Athletes sometimes come from long distances to contend for the prizes. They belong mostly to a caste called Jetti, and are trained from their youth in contests of the kind. Their profession is to injure one another in the presence of persons who are able to pay them for the satisfaction to be derived from this horrible sport, in which both princes and people take infinite delight.

Ordinary blows with the fist, however vigorously applied, would not cause sufficient bloodshed, so before entering the lists the champions put on gloves studded with sharp pieces of horn. They fight almost naked, and before coming to close quarters dance about in threatening attitudes. Then they close furiously, and deal heavy blows on each other's heads with their murderous gloves. Needless to say, blood flows freely. When they have had enough of this, they seize each other round the body and fall struggling to the ground, where they tear at each other like wild beasts.

At intervals they cease fighting to regain breath; but they soon begin again, and the combat does not end until the umpires separate them and one of the two is declared victor. Covered with wounds and literally bathed in blood, they retire and make room for new combatants, who fight with the same ferocity. This spectacle sometimes lasts for hours together, to the great satisfaction of the spectators, who mark their enthusiasm by constant applause. When all is over, the prince distributes among the champions prizes proportionate to the skill and strength which each of them has displayed. The wounds and dislocations of the injured are attended to by men of their own caste, the Jettis being generally very clever in surgery.

At the end of November or the beginning of December the **Deepavali,** feast of lamps, is celebrated. It occupies several days. Every evening while it lasts, the Hindus place lighted lamps at the doors of their houses or hang

paper lanterns on long poles in the street. But as it is held at a time when most of the cereal crops are ready for harvesting, the cultivators in many places are then in the habit of going together in procession to their fields, and there offering to their crops prayers and sacrifices of rams or goats, in order, as it were, to give thanks to their crops for having ripened and become fit for the food of man. Every husbandman also, on three days in succession, proceeds to the dungheap which he has collected for manuring in fields and prostrates himself before it, presenting to it offerings of flowers, lighted tapers, boiled rice and fruits, and begging it humbly to fertilize his lands and to procure him abundant harvests. This worship, it may be remarked, very much resembles that which the Romans used to pay to their god Sterculius.

The **Naga-panchami** is another feast. It is celebrated in the beginning of February in honour of snakes, and especially of the most venomous species, such as the cobra, called naga or nagaraj by the Hindus. This reptile, which is very common and the most dangerous of all, is honoured in a very special manner on this occasion. The people pay visits to the holes where snakes of this sort are generally known to remain concealed, and make offerings to them of milk, plantains, etc.

But the most solemn of all feasts, at any rate in the south of India, is the **Pongal**, which

is also known in some places as the **Maha-Sankranti**[1]. This feast is the occasion of great rejoicing; and the Hindus have two good reasons for regarding it with joy. One is because, the month preceding the Pongul, which is entirely made up of unlucky days, has at last passed; the other is because the month which follows must invariably consist of lucky days.

During the inauspicious month which preceded the Pongul, pandarams, go from door to door about four o'clock in the morning, waking all sleepers by beating their gongs, warning them to be on their guard and to take every precaution against the evil influences of this unlucky period, by appeasing, by means of prayers and sacrifices, the god Siva, who presides over it. With this purpose in view, the women of the house every morning prepare a small patch about a yard square outside the door, smearing it with cow-dung, and tracing several white lines upon it with rice-flour.

They then place within this square several pellets of cow-dung, each adorned with a pumpkin flower. I believe these pellets are supposed to represent Vighneshwara, the god of obstacles, whom they seek to appease by offering him a bouquet. But I do not know why

1. Sankranti is the name given to the first day of the solar month; that is to say, to the day on which the sun passes from one sign of the Zodiac to another. It refers here to its entrance into the sign of Capricorn, a period which the ancients celebrated as that of the re-birth of this bright luminary.

it is that the pumpkin flower is chosen in this case. Every evening these little balls of cow-dung, together with their flowers, are carefully collected, to be kept till the last day of the month. When this day arrives the women, who alone are charged with this ceremony, put them into a new basket, and accompanied by musical instruments and clapping of hands, they solemnly carry them away beyond the precincts of their dwellings and throw them into a tank or some other retired but clean spot.

The Pongal, or Maha-sankranti, always takes place during the winter solstice, the period when the sun, having finished its course towards the southern hemisphere, turns to the north again and comes back to visit the people of India. The feast lasts three days; the first is called **Bhoghi-Pongal,** Pongal of joy,. On this day visits are exchanged between relatives and friends, who make presents and give entertainments to each other; the day passes in diversions and amusements of all sorts.

The second day is called **Surya-Pongal,** Pongal of the sun. In fact the feast appears to be specially dedicated to the sun. The married women first of all bathe with their clothes on, and while still dripping wet put rice to boil In milk on a fire in the open air. As soon as it begins to simmer, they all cry out together, Pongal Pongal! Pongal, Pongal! 'Almost immediately afterwards they remove the vessel from the fire and place it before the idol of Vighneshwara, to whom they offer a portion

of the rice; another portion is given to the cows, and the rest is eaten by the people of the house.

On this day Hindus again exchange visits. On meeting each other the first words they say are: 'Has the rice boiled?' to which the answer is: 'It has boiled.' It is for this reason that the feast is called Pongal in the south of India, the word being derived from Pongedi in Telugu, and Pongaradu in Tamil, both signifying to boil.

The third day is called the **Pongal of the Cows**. On this day they put into a big vessel filled with water some saffron powder, some seeds of the tree called Parati, and some leaves of the margosa-tree. After mixing the ingredients well together, they sprinkle the cows and the oxen with the liquid, walking round them three times. All the men of the house for the women are excluded from this ceremony then turn successively towards the four points of the compass and perform the Sashtanga, or prostration of the eight members, four times before the animals.

The horns of the cows are painted in various colours, and round their necks are hung garlands of green leaves. interlaced with flowers. On these garlands are hung cakes, cocoanuts, and fruits, which, as they are shaken off by the animals, are eagerly scrambled for and devoured, as though they were sacred things, by the crowd following.

The cows are then driven together outside the town or village, and are then made to scatter in all directions by the aid of drums

and noisy instruments. On this day cattle are allowed to graze everywhere without restraint; and no matter what damage they may do in the fields, they, are never driven away.

The idols are afterwards taken from the temples and carried in procession to the sound of music, to the place where the cattle have again been collected. The temple dancing-girls, who are to be found at all feasts and public ceremonies, are not absent on this occasion; they march at the head of the large concourse of people, and from time to time pause to delight the spectators with their dances and songs.

The feast terminates with a performance which, I believe, has no other object than simple amusement, The crowd forms itself into a big circle, in the middle of which a hare is let loose, which in its efforts to escape runs round and round, from side to side, exciting much laughter amongst the spectators, till at last it is caught.

The idols are then carried back to the temples, the cows are led back to the sheds, and thus ends the most popular of all Hindu feasts.

13

Principal Ceremonies

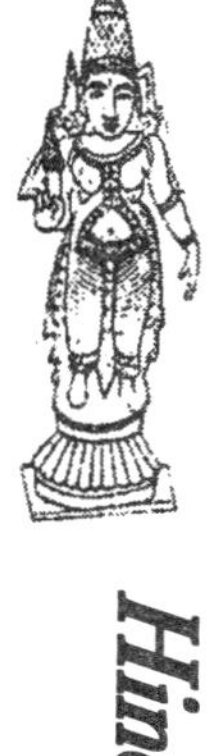

Before entering into more particular details with regard to the ceremonies of the Hindus, it is necessary, to begin by giving an explanation of certain terms pertaining to these ceremonies, and also a short summary of the chief objects aimed at. This sketch will suffice to indicate the tastes and inclinations of the Hindus.

The Samkalpa

The chief preparatory ceremony is the Samkalpa, which means literally resolve of the mind, will, purpose, definite intention, determination, desire. It is no ceremony in itself, but is a prelude to every ceremony.

This method of mental preparation must in no instance be omitted before any religious ceremony. When the Samkalpa has been performed with due meditation, everything that they undertake will succeed; but its omission is alone sufficient to transform all the ceremonies that follow into so many acts of sacrilege which will not pass unpunished. The person must meditate preliminarily on the following points. He must think—

1. Of Vishnu, meditating upon him as the ruler and preserver of this vast universe, as the author and giver of all good things, and as he who brings all undertakings to a successful issue. With these thoughts in his mind he repeats thrice the name of Vishnu, and worships him.
2. He must think of Brahma. He must remember that there are nine Brahmas, who created the eight million four hundred thousand kinds of living creatures, of which the most important is man; that it is the first of these Brahmas who is ruling at the present time; that he will live for a hundred years of the gods[1]; that his life is divided into four parts, of which the first and half of the second are already gone. He must then worship him.
3. He must think of the Avatara, or incarnation, of Vishnu in the form of a white pig, which was the shape in which that deity slew the giant Hiranyaksha. After having thoroughly realized the idea that this Avatara is the most celebrated of all in the Kali-yuga, he worships the pig god.
4. He must think of Manu. He reminds himself that there are fourteen Manus, of which the names are Svarochisha,

1. Each day, according to the reckoning of the gods, is as long as several milliards of years.

Tamasa, Svayambhuva, Raivata, etc., and that they reign over the fourteen worlds during the hundred gods' years that Brahma's life will last. As Vaivaswata Manu is now in power in the Kali-yuga, in which the Hindus are living at this present time, he offers him worship.

5. He must think of the Kali-yuga. He must recollect that we are at present in the early parts of this yuga.

6. He must think of Jambudwipa. This is the continent in which India is situated. He pictures it to himself as surrounded by a sea of salt water, having in the centre a mountain of gold sixteen thousand yojanas[1] high, called Mahameru, on the thousand summits of which the gods have fixed their abode. He must remember that at the foot of this mountain on the east side grows the Jambu-vriksha, a tree which is a thousand yojanas high and as many in circumference; that the juice of the fruits of this tree, which fall of their own accord when ripe, forms a large river which flows towards the west, where it mingles its waters with the rise of the sea; that the water of this river possesses the power of converting everything it touches into gold, for which reason it has been

---

1. The ordinary yojana is about nine miles, but the sacred *yojana*, which is here mentioned, is very much longer.

called the Bangaru-nadi or Golden River. He must not omit to think of this sacred tree, nor yet of the continent of Jambudwipa, where it is situated.

7. He must think of the great king Bharata, who at one time governed Jambudwipa and whose reign forms one of the Hindu eras.
8. He must think of the side of the Mahameru which faces him, that is to say, of the west side of this sacred mountain, if he lives to the west of it, the east, if he lives to the east of it, etc.
9. He must think of the corner of the world called Agnidika, or the Corner of Fire, over which the god Agni-Iswara presides, and which is that part of the world in which India is situated.
10. He must think of the Dravida country, where the Tamil language is spoken.
11. He must think of the moon's pathway, and the change of one moon to another.
12. He must think of the year of the cycle in which he is living. The Hindu cycle is composed of sixty years, each of which has its own particular name. And he must say aloud the name of the particular year of the cycle in which he is living.
13. He must think of the Ayana in which he is. There are two Ayanas in the year, each of which lasts six months — one called

the Dakshina-ayana or southern Ayana, which includes the time during which the sun is south of the equinoctial line, and the other called Uttara-ayana or northern Ayana, which comprises the rest of the year, during which the sun is north of this line. He must pronounce the name of the ayana which is then going on.

14. He must think of the Ritu or season of the year. There are six Ritus in the year, each of which lasts two months. He must pronounce the name of the Ritu in which he is performing the Samkalpa.
15. He must think of the moon. Each moon is divided into two equal parts, one of which is called Sukla-paksha and the other Krishna-paksha. Each of these divisions lasts fourteen days, and each day has its own special name. He must call to mind the division and day of the moon, and pronounce their names.
16. He must think of the day of the week and pronounce the name.
17. He must think of the star of the day. There are twenty-seven in each lunar month, each of which has a name. He must pronounce the name of the one which is in the ascendant on that day.
18. He must think of the Yoga, or conjunction of stars of the day. There are twenty-seven of these, corresponding to the twenty-seven stars, each with its own name. He must pronounce the

name of the Yoga, as also that of the star.

19. He must think of the Karana, of which there are eleven in each lunar month, each with its own name. The same formality must be gone through as the star and the Yoga.

All these diverse objects to which the person must turn his thoughts when performing the Samkalpa are so many personifications of Vishnu, or rather are Vishnu himself under different names. Besides this ordinary Samkalpa, there is another more elaborate one, which is reserved for grand occasions.

This pious introduction to all their ceremonies averts, by virtue of its merits, every obstacle which the evil spirits and giants would put in the way. The name of Vishnu alone, it is true, is sufficient to put them to flight, but nothing can resist the power of the Samkalpa.

Puja[2]

Of all the Hindu rites, Puja is the one that occurs most frequently in all their ceremonies, both public and private, in their temples and elsewhere. Every Hindu is absolutely obliged to offer it at least once a day to his household gods. There are three kinds of Pujas —the great, the intermediate, and the small.

---

1. Puja means honour, respect, homage. worship. —Ed.

The great sacrifice is composed of the following parts:

1. Avahana. The evocation of the deity.
2. Asana. A seat is presented to him to sit on.
3. Swagata. He is asked if he has arrived quite safely, and if he met with no accident on the way.
4. Padya. Water is offered to him for washing his feet.
5. Arghya. Water is presented to him in which flowers, saffron, and sandalwood powder have been placed.
6. Achamana. Water is offered that he may wash his mouth and face in the prescribed fashion.
7. Madhuparka. He is offered in a metal vessel a beverage composed of honey, sugar, and milk.
8. Snana-jala. Water for his bath.
9. Bhooshan-abharana. He is presented with cloths, jewels, and ornaments.
10. Gandha. Sandalwood powder.
11. Akshatas. Grains of rice coloured with saffron.
12. Pushpa. Flowers.
13. Dhupa. Incense.
14. Dipa. A lighted lamp.
15. Naivedya. This last offering is composed of cooked rice, fruit, liquefied butter, sugar and other eatables, and betel.

Before offer of these gifts, care should be taken to sprinkle a little water over them with the tips of the fingers. The worshippers then prostrate themselves before the deity.

For the intermediate puja the last nine articles are offered; for the lesser, only the last six.

When sacrifices of blood are necessary to appease ill-disposed gods or evil spirits, the blood and the flesh of the animals that have been sacrificed are offered to them.

Arati

This ceremony is performed only by married women and courtesans. Widows would not be allowed, under any circumstances, to participate in it.[1]

A lamp made of kneaded rice-flour is placed on a metal disc or plate. It is then filled with oil or liquefied butter and lighted. The women each take hold of the plate in turn and raise it to the level of the person's head for whom the ceremony is being performed, describing a specified number of circles with it. Instead of using a lighted lamp they sometimes content themselves with filling a vessel with water coloured with saffron, vermilion, and other ingredients. The object of this ceremony is to counteract the influence of the evil eye and

1. Widows are not allowed to take part in any of the domestic ceremonies of the Hindus, Their presence alone would be thought to bring misfortune, and if they dared to appear they would be rudely treated and sent away.

any ill-effects which, according to Hindu belief, may arise from the jealous and spiteful looks of ill-intentioned persons.

The Arati is one of the commonest of their religious practices, and is observed in public and private, It is performed daily, and often several times a day, over persons of high rank, such as rajas, governors of provinces, generals, and other distinguished members of society. Whenever people in these positions have obliged to show themselves in public, or to speak to strangers, they invariably call for the courtesans or dancing-girls from the temples to perform this ceremony over them, and so avert any unpleasant consequences that might fire from the baleful glances to which they have been exposed. Kings and princes often have dancing-girls in their employ who do nothing else but perform this ceremony[1].

The Arati is also performed for idols. After the dancing-girls have finished all their other duties in the temple, they never fail to perform this ceremony twice daily over the images of the gods to whom their services are dedicated. It is performed with even more solemnity when these idols have been carried in procession through the streets, so as to turn aside malignant influences, to which the gods are as susceptible as any ordinary mortal.

---

1. Arati is performed also when people take children from one village to another, on visits to relations and friends. —Ed.

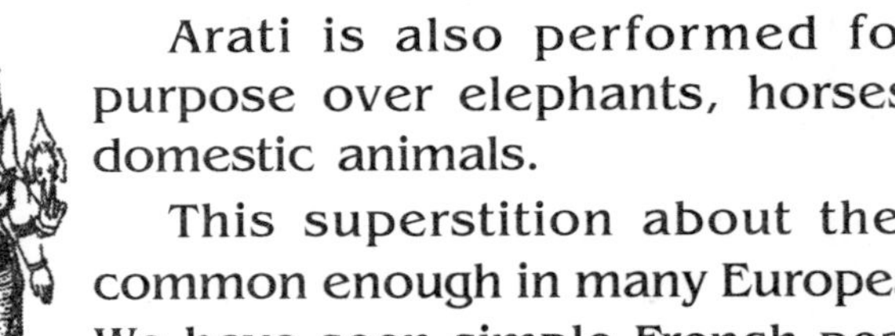

Arati is also performed for the same purpose over elephants, horses, and other domestic animals.

This superstition about the evil eye is common enough in many European countries. We have seen simple French peasants hastily draw their children away from some stranger or ill-looking person, for fear his glance might cast some spell over the little ones. The same notion was prevalent at the time of the ancient Romans.

The Romans too had their god Fascinus, and amulets of the same name were given to children to wear to preserve them from spells of this nature. The statue of the god, placed on the triumphal car, preserved returning conquerors from the malignity of the envious. Hindus call this spell Drishti-dosha, or the evil influence of the eye. And they invented the Arati to avert and counteract it. Their credulity on this subject is boundless. According to them, it is not only the animate objects that come under the influence of the Drishti-dosha; vegetable substances are equally susceptible to it. It is to avert this spell that they stick up a pole in all their gardens and fields that are under cultivation. On the top of this pole they fix a large earthen vessel, well whitened on the outside with lime. This is to attract the attention of malicious persons who may be passing, as it will be the first thing to catch their eye and will thus prevent their spells from producing any disastrous effects on the crops,

which otherwise would certainly be affected by the evil influence.

Akshatas

This is the name given to husked rice coloured with a mixture of saffron and vermilion. There are two kinds of Akshatas, one specially consecrated by mantra, the other simple coloured rice. The first is used when performing puja and in other great ceremonies; the other kind is only a toilet requisite, or is used as an offering of politeness. It is considered good manners to offer some in a metal cup to anyone to whom a ceremonious invitation is sent. The latter in return takes a few grains and applies them to the forehead.

The Pavitram[1]

The object of the Pavitram is to scare away giants, evil spirits, or devils, whose mission it is to bring disasters upon men and mar the ceremonies. The very sight of the Pavitram makes them tremble and take to flight.

This powerful amulet consists of three, five, or seven stalks of darbha grass plaited together in the form of a ring. Before beginning any ceremony the presiding purohit takes the Pavitram, and after dipping it in sanctified water, places it on the ring-finger of his right

1. The Pavitram is made of stalks of darbha grass. It is worn simply as a mark of sanctification. Three stalks are generally used for funeral ceremonies; two for marriage ceremonies and other auspicious occasions. —Ed.

hand. The seeds and oil of sesamum are very nearly as efficacious as the Pavitram; but the grass they call darbha is the most efficacious, for it possesses the virtue of purifying everything that it touches. The brightest can do nothing without it. It is the basis of all those pious and meritorious acts which are known by the generic term of Moksharthas, or deeds which lead to everlasting felicity, and which consist of the Asvamedha sacrifice of the horse, the Vajapeya, the Rajasuya, the Satrayaga, and other kinds of yajnas which are particularly pleasing to Vishnu.[1]

No important action in life can take place without it. That is to say, it is necessary in the Kamyarthas, which include the Garbha-dana, the Jatakarma, the Namakarana, the Annaprasana, the Chaula, the Upanayana, the Simanta, and marriage[1]. It is in frequent use in the various religious exercises of the Hindus pertaining to their four states, namely, Brahmachari, Grahastha, Vanaprastha, and

1. Vajapeya = trial of strength; a kind of soma sacrifice. Satra-yaga = another great soma sacrifice. Rajasuya = royal inaugural sacrifice. —Ed.

2. Kamyarthas = deeds which lead to worldly happiness. Garbhadana = pregnancy. Jatakarma = horoscope writing. Namakarana = naming ceremony. Annaprasana = weaning or food-giving ceremony. Chaula = head-shaving ceremony. Upanayana = initiation of a pupil. Simanta = ceremony of parting the hair, in the case of women six or eight months in pregnancy. —Ed.

Sannyasi. In fact this sacred grass, the purity of which is considered unequalled, appears in every religious or civil ceremony.

Punyaha-Vachana

The literal translation of this word is 'the evocation of virtue,' and it is the name given to the ceremony by which the sacred water is consecrated. They proceed thus: - Having purified a place in the house in the ordinary manner, they sprinkle it with water. Then the officiating Brahmin purohit seats himself with his face to the east, and they place before him a banana leaf with a measure of rice on it. At one side is a copper vessel full of water, the outside of which has been whitened with lime; the mouth of the vessel is covered with mango leaves, and it is placed on the rice. Near the copper vessel they put a little heap of saffron, which represents the god Yogeshwara, to whom they perform puja, and for Naivedya they offer jaggery (raw sugar) and betel. They then throw a little sandalwood powder and Akshatas into the copper vessel, while reciting appropriate Mantras with the intention of turning the water which it contains into the sacred water of the Ganges. Finally, they offer a sacrifice to the vessel, and for naivedya they offer bananas and betel. The water thus sanctified purifies places and persons that have become unclean.

Panchagavya

Panchagavya is made of the five things derived from the cow: milk, curd, ghee, dung and urine, all of which are regarded as holy. This is the way in which it is consecrated: The house is purified in the usual way. They then bring five little new earthen vessels, into one of which they put milk, into another curds, into a third liquefied butter, into a fourth cow-dung, and into the fifth the urine of a cow. These five little vessels are then placed in a row on the ground on some darbha grass, and they perform puja in the following manner:

First, they make a profound obeisance before the deity Panchagavya, and they meditate for some time on its merits and good qualities. Some flowers are placed on the five vessels, and for asana they make the god an imaginary present of a golden seat or throne. They then offer to each vessel, as Arghya, a little water, which is poured round them. For Padya, a little more water is poured out for them to wash their feet, and Achamana is offered immediately afterwards in the same way. The Snana-jala is water in which a little darbja grass has been steeped, which is presented to the god Panchagavya, to enable him to perform his ablutions. The tops of the vessels are then covered with Akshatas, while they are presented, in imagination of course,

with jewels, rich garments, and sandalwood. In conclusion they offer them flowers, incense, a lighted lamp, bananas, and betel as Naivedya, and finally, make another profound obeisance.

These preliminaries ended, the officiating priest addresses the following prayer to the god Panchagavya, or, what is the same thing, to the substances contained in the five vessels: 'O god Panchagavya, vouchsafe to pardon the sins of all the creatures in the world who offer sacrifice to you and drink you, Panchagavya. You have come proceeding from the body of the cow; therefore, I offer you my prayers and sacrifices in order that may obtain the remission of my sins and the purification of my body, which are accorded to those who drink you. Vouchsafe also to absolve us, who have offered you puja, from all the sins that we have committed either inadvertently or deliberately. Forgive us and save us!'

After this prayer they make another profound obeisance and put the contents of the five vessels into one. Then taking this vessel into his hands, the purohit performs the Hari-smarana (meditating on Hari), drinks a little of this liquid, pours a little into the hollow of the hands of all persons present, who also drink it, and keeps the rest for use during the ceremony. Betel is then presented to the Brahmins who are present, after which they disperse.

There is also another rostral preparation called **Pancha-amrita**, which is composed of milk, curds, liquefied butter, honey, and sugar mixed together. It, however, possesses a certain degree of merit under some circumstances.

The Purification of Places

Before the performance of any ceremony the place where it is to take place must be previously purified. This is usually the duty of the women, and the principal ingredients required are cow-dung and darbha grass. They dilute the cow-dung with water and make a sort of plaster with it, which they spread over the floor with their hands, making zigzags and other patterns with lime or chalk as they go on. They then draw wide lines of alternate red and white over this and sprinkle the whole with darbha grass, after which the place is perfectly pure. This is the way in which Hindus purify their houses day by day from the defilements caused by promiscuous goers and comers. It is the rule amongst the upper classes to have their houses rubbed over once a day with cow-dung, but in any class it would be considered an unpardonable and gross breach of good manners to omit this ceremony when they expected friends to call or were going to receive company.

This custom appears odd at first sight, but it brings this inestimable benefit in its train, that it cleanses the houses where it is in use

from all the insects and vermin which would otherwise infest them.

Pandals

All the more important Hindu ceremonies, such as Upanayana, marriages, etc. take place under canopies etc. made of leaves and branches of trees which are erected with much pomp and care in the courtyard or in front of the principal entrance door of the house. The Pandal is usually supported by twelve wooden posts or pillars, and covered with foliage and branches of trees. The top or ceiling is ornamented with paintings or costly stuffs, while the whole is hung with garlands of flowers, foliage, and many other decorations. The pillars are painted in alternate bands of red and white. The Pandals of rich people are often exquisitely decorated. A propitious day, hour, and star are always chosen on which to erect these canopies. Then the relations and friends all assemble to set up the centre pillar, which is called the Muhurta-kal, and to which they offer puja to the accompaniment of music. Under this canopy all the ceremonies connected with the fete take place, and the guests remain underneath it till the end of the performance. The houses of Hindus are not as a rule sufficiently spacious, or in any way well adapted for receiving large numbers of guests, so necessity has suggested this picturesque alternative.

Besides these pandals, which are only used

on grand occasions, upper-class people generally have a permanent one before their principal entrance door to protect from the sun persons who may come to visit them, and who could not with propriety and due regard to custom be invited to come inside.

• • •

Lotus
PRESS